Eyes in a Storm

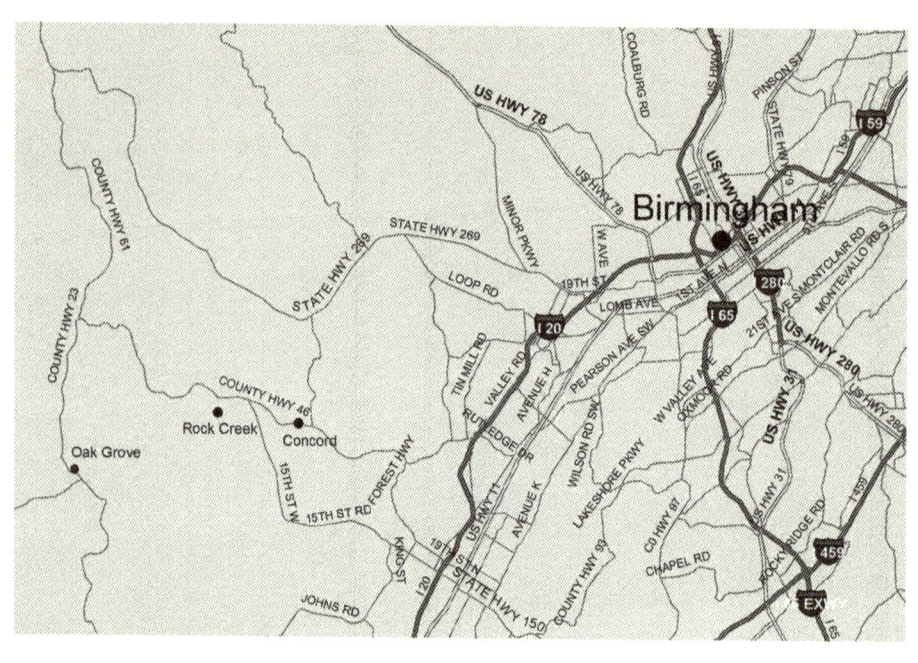

Eyes in a Storm

✦

How One Community Weathered Life After a Deadly Tornado

Jessica Gregg McNew

iUniverse, Inc.
New York Lincoln Shanghai

Eyes in a Storm
How One Community Weathered Life After a Deadly Tornado

iUniverse, Inc.

For information address:
iUniverse, Inc.
2021 Pine Lake Road, Suite 100
Lincoln, NE 68512
www.iuniverse.com

ISBN: 0-595-27706-3

Printed in the United States of America

In memory of Leslie Whittington, Charles Falkenberg, and their daughters, Zoe and Dana, who died in another disaster, the man-made tragedy on September 11, 2001.

Contents

Acknowledgements

I am deeply grateful to Chief Tim Love and the Concord Fire District rescuers who enthusiastically stepped behind this project from the moment I proposed it. Many of them endured numerous interviews, as well as follow-up phone calls and e-mails as I gathered information for this book. Most of them do not consider their efforts to put the tornado behind them noble, but I found the bravery they showed during their struggles after the storm to be what made them so heroic. My only regret is that I could not include all of the rescuers' stories in this book.

I also am indebted to the American Red Cross for giving me the opportunity to spend a year writing about disasters. I feel so fortunate to have worked with Beth Dincin, Ken Jordan, Richard Hoffman, Linda Buschke, and Jennifer Brill, who made me feel truly part of a team. I am grateful for all that they taught me. Ande Miller, Rocky Lopes, Luis Garcia, and Michon Zysman were other shining stars among the many Red Cross workers who guided me from one disaster to another. I also would like to thank Bill Blaul for flipping through his Rolodex in search of eager, young reporters and making the phone call that changed my life, and Vince DiPersio, who I met in Alabama while he was working on a film about the tornado for HBO, and who showed much support for this project.

Eyes in a Storm would have never been written without the guidance of Mindy Wilson, and it would have never been published without the encouragement of Ray Sikorski.

So many of my friends had a hand in this book as well. Barbara Frye sifted through the grammatical errors in an early version of this manuscript. Pat Craig checked a later version and served as a wonderful sounding board. Martha Bristow, Rachel Wallach, Amy Pelsinsky, Cindy Schaeffer, and Matthew Katz gave me valuable comments and moral support. Leslie Dahl, a new friend, created the perfect cover. In addition, Elyse Jennings, Jeannie Gracey-Etgen, and Leslie Tremberth provided the child care that allowed me to finish this project. I am humbled by their generosity.

Finally, I would like to thank my husband Kevin for putting up with the crazy life of a disaster reporter, and especially for providing hope along the way.

Introduction

No one who writes about disasters for a living ever wishes for a story. The stories simply happen. They happen when rains swell rivers until they swallow whole the valleys of homes around them, when lightning snaps into a spark the grasses broiled lifeless during a drought, when hurricanes claim coastlines for their own, and when tornadoes erase communities from a map and people from their families.

They happen because nature continues to wreak havoc with man.

In 1998, there were a lot of disasters for a reporter to cover. Before the year's end, tornadoes would kill 129 people in the United States. That was the highest number of lives lost to these storms since 1974, the year of the Super Outbreak, when a band of tornadoes marauded thirteen Southern and Midwestern states like a guiltless gang of thugs. In the near quarter of a century between 1974 and the deadly storm season of 1998, there was only one other year when more than one hundred people died in tornadoes and that was in 1984.

In 1998, the usual places didn't take hits; Tornado Alley states—Texas, Oklahoma, Kansas, Nebraska, Iowa, Missouri, and Arkansas—remained relatively storm-free, while the Southeast and the Upper Midwest suffered the most. These areas certainly weren't immune to violent storms, but this year the weather held the two regions at its mercy.

Reporters and relief workers shuttled from disaster scene to disaster scene that spring, and nightly newscasts spotlighted one neighborhood after another bombed out by more than one-hundred-mile-per-hour winds. The unchecked, tear-soaked words of scared families wearing their only worldly goods became quotes. People learned the names of towns they had never heard of and would never visit, like Spencer, South Dakota, or Comfrey, Minnesota. Then the out-of-towners went away, and communities across the country were left to rebuild.

This book is the story of one of them.

On April 8, 1998, a massive tornado with winds of more than two hundred miles per hour barreled across central Alabama before most folks had put their kids to bed. Many people knew the storm was coming but that didn't lessen its effects. The twister stayed on the ground for more than a half-hour, mowing down much of what stood in its thirty-mile path. Thirty people lost their lives and 252 other victims were injured. Two of the injured died of their wounds days later. The storm also demolished close to eleven hundred homes, and another one thousand houses sustained damage. A second tornado in what turned out to be a trio of twisters killed two people in nearby St. Clair County as the supercell that spawned these storms sped across the north-central portion of the state and into Georgia.

The Concord Fire District, a rural area of three tucked-away communities more than twenty-five miles west of Birmingham, took one of the hardest hits from the powerful tornado. The district's firefighters, volunteers or part-time workers who lived in the very neighborhoods they protected, rushed into the night to save the lives of their families and friends. These rescuers had decades of training and experience among them. They could shock a heart attack victim back to life, cut a mangled driver from a wrecked car, and stop a spreading brush fire. They were tough in body and soul. They knew that no one called the fire department for joyous occasions. That was what being a firefighter was all about; they ran into the burning buildings that other people ran from. Yet what they went through that night and the months to follow was like nothing they had ever experienced. Long after the emergency sirens shut off that night, the firefighters discovered a hurting that lingered like smoke after a fire. Over the next two years, they struggled to put their lives back together and the tornado behind them. This, it turned out, would be their toughest assignment yet.

We are a nation obsessed with disasters, the perfect storms that fill our movie screens and zap us alive with adrenaline. Only a few miles from where a line of twisters pummeled central Florida in February 1998 and killed forty-three people, thrill-seekers can experience a simulated tornado based on the popular movie "Twister" at Universal Studios' theme park in Orlando. However, we have little understanding of a disaster's long-term effects. We are like a river rising with more rains on the way. Global warming experts predict more volatile weather and deadly disasters as our climate heats up. Even if they are wrong, we continue to place ourselves in harm's way as we stretch our cities and towns into undeveloped countryside, flood plains, precarious coastlines, and landscapes prone to brush fires. Tornadoes can and have occurred in all fifty states. Then there are floods, wildfires, blizzards, hurricanes, and earthquakes; I wrote about twenty types of disaster for DisasterRelief.org.

Most people don't even remember the tornado that struck Birmingham, Alabama, on April 8, 1998. But it severed marriages, hardened souls, and left veteran firefighters wondering if they could ever go to work again without thinking about that night. A disaster of similar magnitude will likely happen every year in some town or city whose residents have the misfortune of literally being in the wrong place at the wrong time. The devastation it will leave in its wake goes way beyond just a few days of headlines.

Part One: Tornado

o o o o o o o o o o o o o o o o o o o o o o o o o o o o o o o o o o

"You don't know what kind of man you are until you're fixin' to die."

—*Captain Terry Hyche*

Eddie Maxwell went to his favorite hill to wait for the tornado.

All day the National Weather Service had issued storm warnings with a frightening staccato regularity, and the clouds churning over Mississippi beckoned him out on a night anyone else would have stayed in. Eddie, a volunteer storm spotter since 1992, knew that much of the severe weather that hit the Birmingham area entered Alabama from Mississippi. After a quick dinner with his wife, Patricia, he loaded the front seat of his GMC Jimmy with his equipment—a police scanner, a ham radio, a video camera, a cellular phone, a fire radio, and his turnout gear, as well as a portable TV to monitor the local weather reports and radar. Then he kissed Patricia and left his Rock Creek home.

On most nights, Eddie could have looked up into an eyeful of stars. Tonight, heavy gray storm clouds crowded them out. The air was swollen with humidity—not an uncommon occurrence for April in Alabama—and Eddie wondered for the first, but not the last time, how the night would end.

He drove west, past the ranchers, the old home places, and the trailers of the rural Concord Fire District in Birmingham's western outskirts. The main road, called Warrior River Road as it snaked through Rock Creek, turned into Lock 17 Road not far from his house. The winding two-lane led him up and over easy rolling hills and beneath trees as tall as office buildings. He drove over Valley Creek and past the fire chief's house and Station Three, the tiny town of Oak Grove's two-story firehouse that the volunteers had built themselves. He sped past an antiques store, a service station, the Grove restaurant, and the Oak Grove School, the area's public school for kindergartners to high-schoolers. Its brick building was a well-known landmark in this part of Jefferson County. Everyone knew someone who graduated from the school, and it was not unusual for multiple generations of the same family to have sat in its classrooms. Twice, bad storms believed to have been tornadoes had struck the school, once in the 1950s, and then again a decade later.

After driving for twenty minutes, Eddie ended up at what he liked to call his vantage point, a hill five miles northeast of Oak Grove that looked like any other hill in central Alabama. Lush and green from the usual early spring rains, the knoll arched away from a countryside with deep pockets of coal that for years had kept men and a few women in Jefferson County's families underground. From this ordinary hill, Eddie could watch clouds roll into the area from Tuscaloosa and Pickens counties, the two counties that lay between Mississippi and his home in Rock Creek. In the six years he had volunteered for the weather service, the vantage point had proven to be the perfect place to spot strong storms before they reached metropolitan Birmingham. If bad weather were to hit that night, Eddie Maxwell would be one of the first to see it.

He knew this area of Alabama almost better than he knew himself. He had grown up in nearby Hueytown, the home of the "Alabama Gang"—race car drivers Davey, Donnie and Bobby Allison, Neil Bonnett, and Red Farmer. He went to work in the coal mines and married his childhood sweetheart. At forty-nine, his white hair gave him a wise, fatherly look that matched his disposition. Five years before that night, he had become a Concord District firefighter after his son did some court-ordered community service work for the department. It was Eddie's way of saying thanks for helping out his boy. He stayed on with the district, because he liked the work and got along well with the other guys. They saw him as the type of fellow who would do whatever he could to help someone out. When one of the other firefighters bought a $1,600 four-wheeler from him, Eddie refused to be paid in full. He knew the young man had two kids and was building a house, so Eddie made him pay only $100 a month until the debt was gone.

That kind of old-fashioned looking out for your neighbors happened all the time in Eddie's community, where families lived for generations and streets bore the names of many longtime residents—Swindle, Hancock, Dates. Most of the district's rescue workers needed only a person's name to respond to an emergency call, for they knew where nearly everyone in the area lived. Residents often dropped by one of the fire stations to get their blood pressure checked or to ask one of the paramedics to examine the bumps and the bruises their kids acquired while skating or playing baseball. Every Christmas, one or two of the firefighters dressed up as Santa Claus and from the top of an engine tossed candy to children in the district's three communities of Concord, Rock Creek, and Oak Grove. Overall, the Concord Fire District had a lot of the small-town traits that Americans idealize. People watched out for each other. They closed deals with a handshake. Parents knew their neighbors well enough even to scold their children, should the need arise. People looked each other in the eye when they greeted them. They were friendly to outsiders, but preferred to rely on the familiar faces around them. Folks might know a family by the church they attended. Most of the houses of worship in these parts were Baptist or Methodist. They were white clapboard or brick buildings with full parking lots every Sunday morning and catchy signs that might read "Free Trip to Heaven, See Inside."

To outsiders, the Concord Fire District was often referred to as "Corncob," because it was so rural and insular. A firefighter might object to being branded by the term, but could joke about his own preference for a rural lifestyle. "You know you're a redneck when your garage is bigger than your house," one of them bragged.

Eddie didn't particularly mind being labeled a good old boy, if it meant living in a place where people knew everybody else and weren't too shy to help out a neighbor. He liked to pitch in and help out, and he knew the weather service was counting on him on this night. Meteorologists relied on spotters like him to verify what the Doppler radar showed them. While radar could tell weather experts when there was a suspicious circulation in a storm system, the advanced technology could not actually determine if there was a tornado on the ground. The eyes and ears of people like Eddie Maxwell turned out to be as important as million-dollar machinery.

Not long after he arrived on the hill, Eddie's police scanner spit out a report from sheriff's deputies at the Oak Grove substation. Trees were down in the area. He relayed that information to the National Weather Service through another amateur radio operator.

On his portable TV, Eddie watched Birmingham meteorologist James Spann telling viewers in Jefferson County to take cover. A tornado was coming. Eddie radioed a fire dispatcher and asked that all Concord personnel be notified that a tornado was headed for the district.

It was shortly before 8 p.m.

Captain Terry Hyche watched the sky above the oaks that surrounded his house in Oak Grove. Thunder rumbled in the distance.

All afternoon, the threat of storms had nagged at Terry, a burly, thirty-five-year-old firefighter with a wide brown mustache and an easy style of talking. He was a polite man who didn't get rattled too easily. In fact, he had lived in Alabama all of his life and had witnessed quite a few bad storms, so tornado warnings usually didn't set him worrying. Still, he couldn't help but notice the flood of weather advisories that afternoon. Plus, he was the captain on duty that night, so he needed to keep track of this approaching storm. Heavy rains caused car wrecks. Downed power lines led to other problems.

In the living room, Terry's two young boys played, and the thick air carried their high-pitched voices to the porch. Terry's wife Kathy and her sister Rachel chatted while they kept an eye on the boys. The family had just returned from dinner at the Good Times Cafe, a few blocks away, and everyone was in a good mood.

Then, over Terry's handheld radio, storm spotter Eddie Maxwell announced in an urgent clip, "A tornado is headed for the Concord Fire District." Thunder still rolled in the distance in low moans and lighting skipped above the treetops. Terry scanned the sky again and considered the situation.

There were forty-three square miles in the Concord Fire District, which he knew was home to five thousand people. Seven miles of main road dipped up and down from Concord on the eastern edge of the district, the closest community to Birmingham, to Rock Creek on the west and then further west to Oak Grove. There was one traffic light on the main road, and it stopped cars at Church Lane in Concord, right by the Concord Baptist Church and the elementary school. Behind both buildings was Station One, the first of three fire stations in the district. It was a nondescript, one-story building that sat across from the community hall and a few, squatty homes where one of the neighbors liked to shoot off his guns from time to time with a rat-tat-tat that could make a firefighter waiting for calls on a quiet day jump with alarm from the plush, hand-me-down sofa in the break room.

Driving west, away from Birmingham, Rock Creek was the next community, a cluster of modest homes with neat front porches, clean yards, and pickups in the driveway. There were a few businesses—Rabbit's Barbecue, KC Racing, where NASCAR hopeful Jimmy Kitchens ran his operation, another restaurant, a video store—and Station Two, an unmanned building that held a fire truck, an engine, and extra equipment for the district. Oak Grove, with its school and restaurant and third fire station, was just a few miles over the hills. Terry and his family lived less than a mile from Station Three.

In all, there were more trees than people in the Concord Fire District, more undeveloped land than subdivisions. If a tornado barreled through its territory, there was a chance it wouldn't tear up anything but oak trees and wild grass. In fact, that's what Terry guessed would happen.

All this hubbub and we're probably in for a quiet night, he figured.

At 8 p.m., a firefighter at Station Three in Oak Grove came on the air to do the nightly radio check. His voice sounded as calm as it had the night before. But up in the sky over the fire station, Terry noticed something odd, a black spot. It was the darndest thing. It looked like a big balloon, a big, black balloon that the lightning danced around but didn't pierce. The air grew heavier around him. Not a leaf moved in the yard.

From the living room, seven-year-old David called out, "Are we going to get hit by a tornado?"

"Nooo," Terry said, drawing out the word. At that moment, he wasn't thinking about the two long-ago storms, believed to have been twisters, which had damaged the school years before. He was thinking that he didn't want his boy to worry. "Ain't no tornado ever hit Oak Grove and ain't one that ever will," he said.

Christie and Matthew Seals lived in an older house that overlooked most of Rock Creek, a one-story, wood-shingled fixer-upper they hoped to remodel and sell in a few years. For now, it was a nice place to raise the kids, out in the country and nestled in the trees. Christie was twenty-eight, a quiet-spoken mother and a woman with the soft figure of someone who's had three babies, but the strong arms of someone who cradles other people's children back to good health. Her short, brown hair waved around her young-looking face, with its blue eyes and full lips. She looked like the kind of person who would be easy to talk to, someone a little child would turn to if he were in pain. She worked the night shift as an intensive care nurse at Children's Hospital in Birmingham and when she came home in the mornings she loved to watch the sunlight stream through the trees as she drove up Hancock Drive to the house. Every day, when she and her two little ones would meet their older brother, Nathan, at the school bus stop at the end of the street, their neighbor, Verlene Williams, would find some excuse to come out to her mailbox and talk to the family. Yes, Christie thought, she and Matthew had picked a great place to raise their children.

They had met years before as neighbors, when eight-year-old Nathan was just a toddler and Matthew was raising his own boy. Christie was finishing up nursing school and worked as a secretary. She liked how good Matthew was with her son, a blond-haired, ruddy-skinned boy who liked to climb trees and to act silly whenever his mama had a camera. In one picture she kept, he stood in front of a lamp so that the shade stood on his head like a hat. In other pictures, he donned costumes or made funny faces. Matthew adored Christie's son and adopted Nathan after the couple married. Then they had two more children together, John Michael, who was two, and Margaret, who was one.

Like all houses with children, theirs was a noisy place, and on this night, the kids were particularly restless. They were waiting out the storm with their mother under a mattress propped like a tent against her bedroom wall. The room was in the center of the house, which Christie knew made it the safest place to be in a tornado. But the kids wanted to be in their own rooms, playing.

In the living room, Matthew watched as TV meteorologist James Spann warned viewers about the storms. Outside the house it was quiet, too quiet for Nathan.

"Mama, can I go change my clothes?" he said.

"No, you stay right here until the storm passes." She smiled at him. "It will be over soon."

It was actually another disaster—a blaze that swept through Concord Baptist Church in 1973—that prompted a group of men in the community to form Concord's fire department. Firefighters from the neighboring towns of Bessemer, Hueytown, and Pleasant Grove worked to put out the massive church fire. But afterward, Concord's residents decided they needed their own volunteer fire department. Two years later, the small community decided to go one step further and residents voted to form a fire district. Every homeowner and business owner within district boundaries was required to pay annual fire dues. The fee would be the same for all residential properties, $120 a year for homeowners in 1998, but would vary for businesses based on size and usage.

Until Station One was built in the late 1970s, firefighters ran calls out of borrowed garages. In 1981, firefighters opened the station in Oak Grove and then added the unmanned station in Rock Creek four years later. By 1998, firefighters covered a forty-three-square-mile area and ran on eight hundred calls a year. Most of them were for emergency medical service, for heart attacks, sick patients, or car accidents.

Like so many rural fire departments did, Concord relied on both paid and volunteer firefighters. There were twelve paid firefighters and about sixty volunteers, a number that dropped during hunting season. Many of the paid men held full-time jobs with larger fire departments in nearby Birmingham, Bessemer, or Hoover. Others worked as paramedics for local ambulance transport companies. Many of the volunteers were like storm spotter Eddie Maxwell, civic-minded residents who liked helping out their community. There was only one woman, Belinda Fitzsimmons, who had once thought she wanted to be a nurse, but became a firefighter and paramedic instead. She held two full-time jobs, at Bessemer Fire Department and at North Star Ambulance Service. Tall and boisterous, with a strong build, perfectly manicured nails, and two small children, she was seen as one tough lady by the other firefighters, although one or two of the good old boys in the community weren't quite sure what to make of her.

The fire district had always been a working class community where people fixed cars, made steel, or mined coal for a living. Most people knew someone who had been or still was a coal miner or steel worker in the two industries that had once been the lifeblood of Birmingham. Jefferson County's Jones Valley was the only place on earth where all three ingredients for iron and steel—coal, ore and limestone—were found in ready abundance. More than a hundred years before, dreams of the riches these resources would bring to the state led a group of wealthy landowners to found the city of Birmingham in the 1870s. The coal and steel industries boomed for decades and Birmingham earned a nickname that stuck, "Magic City." But by the end of the twentieth century, as the demand for U.S. steel declined, jobs in the coal industry plummeted. The University of Alabama at Birmingham and South Central Bell soon became the region's largest employers, but everyone in Concord remembered the days when Birmingham was a company town. Occasionally, an old-timer still called the steel plant TCI, even though Tennessee Coal and Iron had sold the factory to U.S. Steel Corporation decades ago.

With so many residents traveling into Birmingham for work, the district could be a quiet place during the day. There were no mayors and no town councils in Concord's three communities; the only elected officials served on the fire district's board of directors. Because of this, the fire stations had become like town halls. Anybody who wanted to know about a lost dog or a closed road, anybody who wanted to talk politics or to gossip, and anybody who wanted to complain stopped in Station One or Three, where they would more than likely find somebody willing to listen. Quite often, the only people a resident could turn to for help were the firefighters.

Although violent storms were expected for the Southeast on April 8, the day had started quietly enough at the National Weather Service's Birmingham office. At 1 p.m., meteorologists launched a weather balloon from their office at the Shelby County Airport to measure the temperature, humidity, air pressure, and wind speed and direction. The information confirmed that severe storms were likely, and the data were sent to the Storm Prediction Center in Norman, Oklahoma, which monitors severe weather as it develops across the country. Still, there was no panic. In fact, a class of five-year-olds touring the weather service office watched the launch and applauded as the six-foot by three-foot balloon rose into the air. It was a very kindergarten moment. A *Wall Street Journal* reporter based in Atlanta also was at the weather service office that day to research a story on Doppler radar.

It was a good topic to write about. In the past decade, as the weather service increasingly relied on new and improved technology, Doppler radar had become a mainstay of the service's forecasting, as well as television weather reports. The radar's antenna sends out a signal that bounces off rain and then returns to its source. The amount of time it takes for the radar to transmit a pulse or backscatter off the rain, and return to the radar antenna determines the location of the rain and its intensity. The more signals return, the more rain there is. In the same way, the radar can measure the speed of air moving toward and away from the antenna.

On computer screens at the National Weather Service, the data is displayed for meteorologists to interpret. Rain and wind moving toward the radar show up in patterns of blue or green. Rain and wind moving away from the radar are indicated in red. Green and red markings next to each other tell a meteorologist that there is receding motion next to approaching motion, the signature of a mesocyclone, a storm that can spawn tornadoes. The tighter the green and red markings are, the stronger the storm is likely to be. A hook-like shape, formed when the red and green markings nearly wrap around each other, is particularly ominous.

In the 1990s, improved Doppler radar dramatically increased the amount of warning time residents had to seek shelter before a tornado hit. But there was one drawback. Because the technology could pinpoint so readily the conditions necessary for the development of a severe mesocyclone or tornado, it often led to false alarms. What looked like a developing tornado-producing supercell on a radar screen many times could just as easily devolve into typical thunderstorm activity that caused little to no damage. In 1997, the National Weather Service issued eighty-six tornado warnings for the Birmingham area—many for the same storms as they traveled through different counties—but there were only four tornadoes that year. Still, Doppler's flaws were less of an invalidation of the radar system than proof of what a young science the study of tornadoes was.

Even with recent advances, tornadoes remained an enigma and meteorologists couldn't say for sure why some storms spawned funnel clouds and others did not. The more they studied the phenomenon, the more questions they had, and at the end of the twentieth century, the answers remained in the clouds. The basic science behind storms was that they occurred in a warm, moist, and most importantly, unstable atmosphere. A patch of warm air rose above the surrounding air and remained buoyant. Sometimes turbulence at the front of an arriving cold front caused a storm. The front's cold air pushed warm surface air up and storm clouds formed. Some clouds rained themselves out. Others grew into supercells, cloud masses that dumped rain and unleashed lightning and often hail. At their worst, they spun out twisters.

Although Alabama was not as tornado-prone as Texas or Oklahoma, the state's climate made it hospitable to storms. They fueled themselves with warm, water-saturated air from the Gulf of Mexico. Every Alabama native, it seemed, carried a memory of taking cover from a tornado, usually a small one that tore branches from a tree or rocked a mobile home.

But over the years, tragedy had spun through the state as well. On March 21, 1932, multiple tornadoes killed more than 270 people in central Alabama in less than six hours. Birmingham, Tuscaloosa, Demopolis, Montgomery, Alexander City, and Anniston all suffered under the fierce winds. At least two supercells spawned the deadly storms and there was evidence that tornadoes raked the same areas more than once. A more exact death toll was hard to come by; many of the African Americans who lost their lives simply were not counted.

On April 3, 1974, four powerful tornadoes and at least four weaker ones stormed through Alabama, killing eighty-six people and injuring 949 other victims. The storms terrorized sixteen counties in the state, including Jefferson County, where a touchdown in the Concord Fire District damaged homes, but mercifully took no lives. A monster tornado struck the town of Newburg in Franklin County at 6:30 p.m. and wiped out nearly everything in an eighty-five mile path that led it through Lawrence, Limestone, and Madison counties. The towns of Tanner, Harvest, and Hazel Green took brutal beatings from the winds. A second tornado on a twenty-mile tear of destruction took a similar path through Limestone County. Rescue workers trying to help victims of the first tornado found themselves running for cover. Within just a half-hour, the two tornadoes rampaged through several of the same communities.

Alabama was not the only state suffering under deadly weather that day in 1974. In sixteen hours' time, 148 tornadoes touched down in thirteen states. In addition to Alabama, Georgia, Illinois, Indiana, Kentucky, Michigan, Mississippi, North Carolina, Ohio, South Carolina, Tennessee, Virginia, and West Virginia were struck in what came to be known as the Super Outbreak. The storms claimed the lives of 330 people and injured 5,484 other victims in more than twenty-five hundred miles of destruction. From end to end, the devastation could have stretched from North Carolina to California.

Weather experts knew that equally mighty tornadoes would strike again, but they hoped that disasters like the Super Outbreak would never again take as many lives. They believed that improvements in storm prediction, as well as in communications, would make a difference. They looked for new ways to notify the public of severe weather, and the National Weather Service created the expert position of warning meteorologist.

For the most part, Alabama became more storm-ready. Then, a tornado killed twenty church worshippers in Piedmont on April 3, 1994. It was Palm Sunday and congregants at the Goshen United Methodist Church never heard the funnel cloud coming until what sounded like the roar of a train was upon them. A warning had been issued twelve minutes before the storm struck Piedmont, but by then the Goshen congregation was rejoicing at the start of its holiest week of the year. Whole families perished in the disaster and the church's minister lost her four-year-old daughter.

The disaster epitomized Alabama's history with storms. As used to tornadoes as residents were, when the big ones hit they took more lives and left more injuries. Overall, Alabama experienced fewer twisters than most states in Tornado Alley, but had more storm-related deaths and injuries than all but three states.

From 1950 to 1994, Texas saw the highest number of tornadoes, 5,490, followed predictably by two other Tornado Alley states, Oklahoma with 2,300, and then Kansas with 2,110. Alabama did not even crack the top ten. Eight hundred and eighty-six tornadoes in forty-four years left the state ranked fourteenth. Yet, it had the fourth highest number of tornado-related deaths in the nation, with 275 fatalities, and the third highest number of injuries, with 4,483 wounded. Only Texas, Mississippi, and Arkansas had higher death rates. The latter two, like Alabama, saw relatively few storms. Mississippi ranked twelfth and Arkansas ranked sixteenth for the number of storms from 1950 to 1994. Fewer storms might have marauded the Southeast, but they still left behind deadly legacies.

Alabama's topography was partly to blame. Unlike Texas and Oklahoma, Alabama had plenty of rolling hills and towering trees that made storms difficult to spot until they were close enough to be life threatening. Those same giant trees made for deadly weapons, smashing homes and crushing lives when the winds rocked them to the ground. Also, few people had storm shelters in their homes. Some didn't even have basements, and mobile homes, the worst place to be in a tornado, remained a common housing option. Even the average brick home in Alabama wasn't as sturdy as the average brick home in Oklahoma, where builders took into account the common occurrence of thirty-mile-per-hour winds. In Birmingham, thirty-mile-per-hour winds were a rarity. Also, when storms hit at night or in the early morning, it was harder to warn a sleeping public about the danger, and it was obviously more difficult to spot a storm in the dark.

Finally, the fact that Alabama wasn't in Tornado Alley actually put the state at a disadvantage. Sure, tornadoes were common in the Heart of Dixie. But in 1998 no one ever expected the same kind of massive storm that nearly wiped out the town of Jarrell, Texas, just the year before, even after the 1994 tragedy in Piedmont. Part of that was human nature. On the East Coast, beach lovers built houses along the coast of the Atlantic, watched a hurricane wipe them out and then rebuilt in the same spot, thinking, "We've been hit once by disaster, it won't happen again. Lightning doesn't strike the same place twice." Disaster victims commonly tell reporters they didn't believe it could happen to them. Many Alabamans affected by the April 1998 storm felt the same way.

Seven hours after launching the weather balloon on April 8, weather service meteorologists in Birmingham gasped at what they saw on their Doppler radar screens shortly before 8 p.m.—a wide pattern of green and blue against red, the markings of a supercell developing in the skies to the west of Jefferson County, not far from Oak Grove. A tornado warning already had been issued for neighboring Pickens County, but there had been no reports of tornado activity there. At 7:43 p.m., someone from the Tuscaloosa County Emergency Management Agency called to report downed trees. A few minutes later, the multicolored markings on the radar screen swirled together into a fateful hook. The weather service immediately issued a tornado warning for Jefferson County. Ten minutes later, radar showed the telltale hook moving across the county line and into the Concord Fire District.

Captain Terry Hyche couldn't take his eyes off the black spot in the sky. It was so strange. All around the house, lightning flashed again and again. But it never speared that spot. The black ball moved closer and closer toward the house and then what looked like clouds of gray smoke spun sideways through the air. Terry watched the winds bend a tree until its top touched the ground. Then the lights snapped dark and a whistle moaned, a low-pitched whistle that was louder than it should have been. Dread washed over him. The black cloud he had been staring at was a tornado.

"Get down! Everybody get down!" He shouted and ran into the house. Then he switched on his handheld radio and called out to the other firefighters, "There's a tornado on the ground in Oak Grove."

"Is it headed this way?" his wife, Kathy, yelled.

"It's here!"

In seconds, Terry and sister-in-law Rachel dragged a mattress from David's bed into the hallway in the center of the house. Then Kathy and Rachel hugged the two boys to them and Terry covered them with the mattress, diving under it at the last minute. Quickly the whistle outside pitched to a piercing buzz, and Terry had to shout over it to be heard. A sharp pinching in his ears told him the air pressure had dropped. His radio was pressed to his ear and he heard a firefighter at Station Three say that the station had been hit and that he was hiding in a compartment of the rescue truck.

Without even thinking, Terry pulled the radio to his mouth and shouted, "There's a tornado on the ground in Oak Grove. We need all the ambulances you can send."

Back at Station One in Concord, a firefighter heard the message and put out an urgent call to the neighboring fire departments. He knew Terry Hyche was a cool-headed man who wouldn't call for help if he didn't need it. What worried him more was that he could hear the storm's winds howling around the captain as he yelled into his radio.

Huddled next to Terry, Kathy was terrified. She had never heard such fear in her husband's voice. Why was he asking for ambulances, she wondered. How big was this storm?

Outside, the steady buzz burst into black noise, a roaring and screaming squadron of jets. It swallowed the house and surrounded them until they couldn't hear the screams coming from their own mouths. Then there were other sounds. Glass broke. Tree limbs cracked against the side of the house. Now the black noise sounded like a mower as it chewed up pieces of wood and glass and siding and spit them out against the house.

An oak tree smashed through the roof and punctured the ceiling of David's bedroom. Seconds later, tree limbs crashed through the bathroom on the other side of the hall. Only a little slice of roof remained above where the family crouched under David's tiny mattress. Branches and pieces of board rained into the rooms cracked open to the sky. The house shook.

"My God, we're not going to make it," Terry thought. "Any second, the roof above us is going to cave in."

And then there was silence, pure, clear silence that felt as deep as a gasp of air to someone smothering, but lasted only as long as a quick breath. Then the driving rains started.

On the hillside, storm spotter Eddie Maxwell heard shouts from his fire radio. It was Scott Swindle at Station Three. But Eddie couldn't make out what Scott said. The fear and adrenaline in his voice garbled the message. Scott hollered again and then his words were clear: Station Three had been destroyed by the tornado.

Suddenly Eddie was scared. The tornado already had hit Oak Grove. That meant if it followed the typical pattern that storms did through Jefferson County, it would soon reach the hillside where he was parked. But there was no place safe for him to go, no building where he could take cover, no ditch where he could hide. Worse, if he left the hill, he would likely drive right into the storm. He was trapped.

"I could die tonight," he said out loud. "I could die." He picked up his cell phone and called his wife back in Rock Creek. Patricia had been his childhood sweetheart and his wife of twenty-six years. He told he loved her and asked her to go into the basement. "This is big and it's going to make national news," he said.

Patricia knew that he didn't exaggerate and did what he told her, thinking as she walked down the stairs into their basement that she might never hear her husband's voice again. She folded her hands in prayer. "Please God, take me, too, if you have to take Eddie," she asked. "I won't be able to live without him."

Back on the hillside, it was still and quiet. Eddie put on his turnout coat and firefighter's helmet, although he knew they couldn't save him from a tornado. Moments later, strobe-like lightning ignited the sky around him and he watched hail the size of dimes and nickels fall from the clouds. The width of the stones often indicates the strength of the storm's updraft, and the size of this hail squashed any uncertainty Eddie had about the storm's force: It would be powerful.

Moments later, he gasped when he saw it for himself—a wall of green-black clouds that was three-quarters of a mile wide in some places. There was no telltale funnel, just a bank of black that smothered the sky. He watched the storm move through woods east of Oak Grove until it came out in front of him.

His heart stopped beating in his ears. The tornado wasn't taking the path of most storms. It wasn't going to hit the hillside. Eddie wasn't going to die.

He kept his eyes on the clouds as they moved through the woods and then his ease slipped away. The storm was headed for Rock Creek, for his own house, right where Patricia was. He had to get home to save her. He didn't know if he could beat the storm to Rock Creek. But he had to try.

In the living room of his family's home, Matthew Seals heard a frightening rush of sound, like a train or some sort of loud engine. In a horrible instant, he realized it was the storm coming down Hancock Drive.

"Get down! Get down! The storm's coming!" He waved Christie and the three children to the floor under the mattress.

"Should I cut off the lights?" Christie asked.

"It's not going to matter," he shouted and motioned for her to get down on the floor.

Christie didn't understand. Then she heard the roar. It was the loudest noise she had ever heard and suddenly she felt sick. She pressed her head to the floor, and still it got louder and louder until she thought her head would burst. Wind filled the house and what felt like the fingers of a huge hand scooped everything up. Christie flew through the air and felt herself spinning around and around. She lost sight of the children, of Matthew, of their home. Then she felt herself drop.

"I'm going to die," she thought. "And it's going to hurt so much."

Part Two: Rescue

o o o o o o o o o o o o o o o o o o o o o o o o o o o o o o o o o o

"That whole night was nothing but one horrific scene after another. The minute you were convinced that it couldn't get no worse…you'd walk up on something that was a whole lot worse."

—*Firefighter Curtis Poe*

In Rock Creek, Christie Seals lay on the ground about sixty feet from what once was her house and about 250 feet from where the tornado had crushed its pieces into the ground. She was unable to move. When the storm hit Rock Creek, the tornado tore apart the house and then scattered everyone inside. She flew through the air, thinking she was going to die, and then hit the ground. Her leg crumpled under her and she knew it was fractured badly. Pain stabbed her chest. Her split-second nurse's diagnosis told her she had cracked ribs, maybe even punctured a lung. She would need a chest tube and some X-rays as soon as possible. Her body throbbed with pain.

Above her, lightning stalked the neighborhood in menacing flashes. The tornado was miles away, dying a slow death, but forty-mile-per-hour gusts still rolled over her. When the winds ebbed a bit, she could feel someone's cold skin under her fingers. Her eyeglasses had managed somehow to stay on, but she couldn't see through the rain smears on the lenses. By touch alone, she wasn't sure whose body her hand rested on or even if that person was dead or alive. Then she heard a breath, a small gasp, the wheezing sound of someone critically injured. She thought her heart would stop.

It was her eight-year-old son Nathan lying next to her. His shirt was pulled up and her hand rested on his naked stomach. His right arm was underneath the arch of her back. He took a few breaths and then gurgled. He was not conscious, she could tell, and she figured he had suffered some kind of head injury. They would have to get help for him immediately.

"Matthew!" As she called out for her husband, her mind whirled. Where was the rest of her family? My God, were they dead?

"Christie, I can't move my legs." Her husband's thin and strained voice came only a few feet from where she clung to Nathan. Matthew was flat on his back and thought a piece of the house had landed on him. Christie couldn't see him from where she lay. But when she heard that he was immobile immediately she thought, "He's paralyzed." Each of them had been thrown more than fifty feet and she guessed that he had broken his back.

"It will be all right," she called out him. "We'll get help soon."

In her mind, she worked triage. Nathan had the most severe injuries, then Matthew. Hers were not nearly as bad as theirs. But where were their babies?

"John Michael! Margaret!" Pain spread through her chest as she shouted their names into the night.

Nothing.

Then to her right and down a little ways, she heard crying. She recognized two-year-old John Michael first and then one-year-old Margaret. From the direction of their wails, she could tell they weren't more than a few feet away from each other. That was good. If they couldn't see her or their daddy, maybe they could see each other.

"Hold still and don't go anywhere, babies. I love you," she called out.

Ten minutes after eight, Eddie Maxwell sped to Rock Creek and his wife. As he crossed the stream that gave the community its name, rain pounded the road in a heavy downpour. Over his police scanner, he heard a sheriff's deputy call out that winds had blown a tree onto his car in front of Union Hill Baptist Church. That was two blocks from Maxwell's home on Hillview Drive. Maxwell prayed that his wife was all right.

Back at the couple's home, Patricia huddled with neighbors in the basement. There were four parents and three children, the parents locking their arms around the children to cradle them from the impact. As the winds rattled the house, Patricia could feel the basement floor vibrate and her bones shake. Like Eddie, she prayed. She prayed that he would be all right, that their twenty-six years together would not be all that they would have, that the children she covered would not be hurt.

Minutes later, Eddie Maxwell reached Rock Creek. As he turned onto Hillview Drive, he saw a gap where a three-foot-wide oak tree once sheltered the road. Other toppled trees blocked the couple's driveway and littered the yard. A roof rafter speared the window of their car. A bird without feathers lay motionless on the ground.

"My God, Patricia's dead," Eddie thought.

But the house still stood. Its gutters were missing, its shingles were torn off and a rocking chair was wrapped around one of the porch posts.

"Patricia! Patricia!" Eddie ran in the front door shouting. So much adrenaline coursed through his body that he felt he could have dug her out of the basement if he had to.

She met him in the front hallway, alive and crying. Eddie wrapped his arms around her and cried, too. The neighbors came up behind them. Everyone was all right. For the first time that night, the storm spotter made a prayer of thanks.

Once again, Captain Terry Hyche looked up into the dark night, but this time it was from underneath the fifteen-foot gash in his roof, cut by a wide oak. The tree had damaged his son's bedroom and a bathroom, and the storm's winds had flattened a garage that he had spent four years building, saving along the way for each step of construction. The house's kitchen, pantry, and a deck were beat up as well. Broken glass from a window covered the living room floor.

"God, how did you spare us?" he wondered. The radio he still clutched in his hand squawked, and Terry forgot about his own losses for a second as a firefighter relayed the message that Station Three was on the ground. On the ground, he thought. What did that mean? How bad was the damage to the building?

Terry could feel his heart pump faster, like it did whenever he jumped in the ambulance and switched on the siren. He knew this storm was a bad one and that his family wasn't the only one hit. There were injuries for certain, and more than likely, some fatalities. He was the captain on duty and he had to get to the station.

"I got to go," he told Kathy, who was hushing their upset boys. "The station's been hit. There's going to be a lot of folks that's injured. I got to go."

Tears washed down her round face. "No," she begged him. "Please don't go." They had no idea what lay outside the house. What if he stepped on a power line or got trapped in a house? How could she know that he wouldn't get hurt? She had been a firefighter's wife for a long time. She knew the risks and the responsibilities Terry had. But just this once, she begged him, just this once, please stay.

Terry looked at his wife. Her hands shook. Her face was red. She couldn't catch her breath she was so upset. He had never seen her this unnerved. This was a situation he never thought they would be in, a situation that left him with the worst possible decision—to abandon his family or to abandon his duty. He loved Kathy and their boys. But how could he turn his back on people who needed his help? He had made a promise to serve his community. How could he back down from that?

"I'm sorry," he told Kathy. He didn't want to leave, but he had to go. Surely, she would understand that. "I'm sorry."

She wiped the tears from her face with the palms of her hands, but she wouldn't look at him. Finally she sighed and said, "OK."

Terry nodded and told himself he would make it up to her.

With a flashlight in hand, Kathy's sister Rachel ran through the rain to a neighbor's house to find out if the family could stay there. Then she ran back to gather up the boys and some supplies for the night. Terry ducked into his truck and prayed that his family would be OK. He thought he was doing the right thing, but as he started the truck he wondered why it felt like he was abandoning his wife and kids.

He drove only two blocks before he slammed on his brakes. Downed power lines blocked his path. The station was only two more blocks away, so he grabbed his radio from the seat next to him and started on foot, his head lowered against the driving rain. He hadn't walked far in the night when a voice startled him.

"Is it over?"

He wiped his wet face and squinted at the roadside where a tall pine tree rested flat in a ditch. A woman in nightclothes leaned out from under its tree limbs. Three wet and scared children shivered with her. There was no sign of their house.

"Yes," he told them. "It's over." Then he asked, "Are y'all OK?"

They were fine. None of them had any injuries, but their house was gone.

"Go over to Mr. Franklin's and stay there and get your kids dry," Terry told the mother.

"I don't know Mr. Franklin," she said.

"Tell him Terry Hyche sent you."

There was nothing more the firefighter could do for her. He had to get to the station. He wished the woman luck and then he kept on his way. But as he trudged through the night, he realized that of the two houses he had seen so far, his own was badly damaged and this woman's was blown away.

"This could be worse than I imagined," he thought.

In front of him, fallen power lines curled over the road like spaghetti noodles. Everything smelled wet. Terry's rain-soaked T-shirt and pants stuck to him and his boots held inches of water. There were landmines everywhere—hot power lines and tree limbs, mainly—that threatened to trip his every step. At one point, there were so many trees on the road he had to trudge through a wet field. Finally, he reached the station. Before he saw anything, he heard a hissing sound and smelled gas fumes that were so heavy they filled the air like the afternoon's humidity.

"We're all going to be burned to death," Terry thought.

The black clouds that had blotted the sky were gone, and the night had turned eerily light. It was then that Terry took a good look at Station Three, and for the first time, he understood the radio message.

The two-story, steel-framed building was almost completely gone. The storm had blown its siding into a pile of debris across the road and collapsed its steel beams like bendable straws on top of the engine and tanker. A six-ton rescue truck was six feet from where it had been parked, pushed into the front corner of what had been the station. Scott Swindle, the lone firefighter on duty at the station, had hidden in the truck. He wandered around the building's remains, stunned to be alive.

Around the station, the scene was equally shocking. Bent utility poles and one-hundred-year-old oak trees blocked Lock 17 Road, the country two-lane that ran through the town. In fact, it was impossible to see across the road. Thunder still rumbled to the east, toward Birmingham, and rain turned the ruined, roof-less houses into giant gutters. The Oak Grove School looked like it had been bombed. Brick walls buckled outward. Blinds dangled from empty window frames. Pieces of desks were scattered everywhere. The elementary school was destroyed completely and the damage to the high school was extensive.

The storm blew away the school's gymnasium, where a group of twelve cheer-leaders had been practicing only moments before the winds roared through the community. As the tornado hit, the cheerleaders ran from the gymnasium into the lobby, which withstood the winds in large part because of its thick concrete pillars. Glass from the lobby's trophy cases shattered throughout the room. But the awards inside the case were not even dented. Scared and crying, the cheer-leaders huddled together while they waited for help. Had the cheerleaders remained in the gym, they could have been killed. Had the storm hit hours ear-lier, Terry found himself thinking, his own kids and his neighbors' children might not have survived either.

Standing where Station Three once stood, Terry reviewed the situation with Scott Swindle. Most of their equipment was gone. The debris on Lock 17 Road would make it impossible for an ambulance to travel and without a stretcher it would be hard to carry any of the patients to safety. The district's fire chief, Tim Love, radioed the pair several times from his home about a mile away and they gave him a quick report on the situation. He told them he was on his way.

Back at Station One in Concord, a firefighter listened to the messages between Terry and Chief Love and put out several calls for assistance to neighboring fire companies. Rescue workers from nearby Hueytown Fire Department and Ameri-can Medical Response ambulance service were on their way. When help arrived, it would be desperately needed. By then, people hollered for paramedics from houses up and down Lock 17 Road, their voices a chorus of otherwise lonely cries in the rain.

As the rains in Rock Creek turned heavy and beat down in merciless strokes that soaked Christie Seals to her broken bones, she played through the horror that she could not see: Nathan had a serious head injury and had to get help soon. Mat-thew likely had a broken back and could be paralyzed. The two little ones couldn't tell her what was wrong, but they probably suffered broken bones and other injuries. She couldn't move herself or do anything to treat them. All she could do was yell for help. She took as deep a breath as she could inside her bruised chest and shouted, "We need an ambulance here!"

She shouted again and again, ignoring the knife slice through her ribs every time she called out. Her clothes were torn, and the rain pricked her bare skin like needles. Yellow lightning snapped around the family, and the air surged with electricity. Christie felt sure it would kill them. "That would be something," she thought, "to live through a tornado and then be struck by lightning."

In each flash, she saw shreds of insulation, bits of siding, broken furniture. But she couldn't tell how far the devastation stretched. She didn't want to move too much for every time she took a breath, her chest throbbed, and she began to wonder if she suffered more than broken ribs, if the storm had fractured some of her vertebrae. She tried to hold herself as straight as she could and to not move if she could help it, to immobilize her spine like a paramedic would have done by putting a cervical collar around her neck and strapping her to a backboard.

"Help! We need an ambulance!" she called again and again. Still, no one answered. There were no signs of life beyond her family.

Christie began to pray. It came naturally to her. Raised a Methodist, she believed in a functional, purposeful God, one who was real. To her, he was like a light. "If you are in a room, you know whether the lights are on or off," she often said. God was the one who told her to become a nurse when she was a single mom, struggling to figure out what to do with her life. As she drove by a community college one day, she heard his voice telling her to go inside and sign up for some classes. Now she begged him, "Please, please send us help soon." And then later, "Soon for you may not be soon enough for us."

Time passed; later she would learn that it was more than an hour. Finally, she heard her neighbor Mike Calma.

"Are you OK?" he shouted.

"No!" she called back.

"Where are the kids? Are the kids OK?"

"John Michael and Margaret are OK. But Nathan's not OK. We need an ambulance. Call for an ambulance."

"We can't. There are no phone lines. Everything is gone. We're going to have to walk to get help."

Christie caught a sob in her throat. She couldn't, she wouldn't cry. She needed to stay calm for her family. But if her neighbors had to walk to get an ambulance, help was a long way off.

"Please hurry," she begged Mike, although she knew he would do the best he could.

Rain continued to pelt them and lightning lit up the sky all around the hillside. Christie could no longer hear John Michael or Margaret. Were they still there? She was afraid they had gotten up and were walking through the debris.

"John Michael, Margaret, don't move. You're going to be all right. We're going to come get you babies." Her voice squeaked out in painful snatches.

Next to her, she felt Nathan tense up in a seizure. She waited to hear him breath again, holding her own breath as she willed him to live. Finally, she heard another pained gasp. He was alive, but she knew there was nothing she could do to stop him from dying. She was so helpless. If her leg wasn't twisted up under her, if her chest didn't hurt so much, she could have gotten up and fixed his injuries. She had no equipment to work with, but she could have tried to carry him to safety. At the very least, she could have held him in her arms. But there was nothing she could do but wait and pray.

She begged for God's help again. She believed that he could hear her, but as she lay on the ground praying, she wondered if even he could help.

Anyone in Birmingham who had the luck of not losing his electricity and who turned on their fire scanner that night could have heard the following in the hour after the tornado hit:

A report that Station Three in Oak Grove had been destroyed.

A call for ambulances and medical equipment on Lock 17 Road.

Reports of damage on Miller Drive and Stephens Circle in Rock Creek.

A report that Station Two in Rock Creek, as well as Assistant Chief Robbie Miller's home, had been destroyed.

Reports of serious injuries, some life threatening, on Old Rock Creek Road, Dons Drive, Hancock Drive, and Rock Creek Lane.

A call from a firefighter for an ambulance on Hancock Drive.

Twenty minutes later, a second call from the same firefighter and a short, heated exchange. "Are you going to send me some help or not!" "You'll get it when I get it!"

A request for a front-end loader to remove the large section of a house blocking Warrior River Road in Rock Creek.

And, more calls from ambulances and medical equipment in that area.

Through these radio reports and pleas, a picture began to emerge of what firefighters faced. A tornado had plowed through two-thirds of the district, wiping out the Oak Grove School, two fire stations, and whole streets of homes. In Oak Grove, telephone poles, siding, utility wire, and other debris halted traffic on Lock 17 Road, just east of Station Three and the Oak Grove School. In Rock

Creek, everything stopped as Lock 17 Road wound east to Auburn Lane. Then, for more than a mile, there was no passage, as pieces of homes and fallen trees kept the road closed through the heart of the community. An unknown number of people in Oak Grove and Rock Creek suffered from serious injuries. The number of dead couldn't even be estimated.

As if all of this wasn't tragic enough, all of the rescue equipment in Station Two and Station Three had blown away. There were no stretchers or backboards to carry the injured to safety. No flashlights, bandages, splints, or medication. Ninety percent of the district's equipment was gone. The firefighters didn't even have turnout jackets or helmets, the fireproof clothing that protected them on every call. The fire engine and rescue truck that sat in Station Two were destroyed. Gone as well was an antique pumper. Two other pieces of equipment, both tankers, were badly damaged and unusable. Of the eleven pieces of fire apparatus the district owned, only the three at Station One weathered the storm.

Soon, it grew dark, and there was no electricity in any of the damaged areas. The firefighter who manned the radio at the undamaged Station One put in more calls for help to all the neighboring fire departments. One by one, every one responded. Firefighters from Adger, Bessemer, Birmingport, Dora, Fairfield, Hoover, McAdory, Rockyridge, Rolling Hills, Shelco, and Summiton fire departments sent the workers they could spare to help. Hueytown fire and police departments dispatched all of its on-duty personnel, its fire chief, and its mayor, and nearby Bessemer Fire Department sent two crews to Hueytown to fill in. Deputies from the Jefferson County Sheriff's Department arrived to help search for bodies, and three transport companies—American Ambulance Response, North Star Ambulance Service, and RPS Ambulance Service—sent paramedics, medical supplies, and all the ambulances they could. Every person and every piece of equipment would be needed.

Within the next hour, rescue workers set up a command post in Oak Grove and at race car driver Jimmy Kitchens' shop in Rock Creek. KC Racing was the biggest building still standing and one of the few that still had electricity. A line of ambulances in front of the race car shop awaited patients. Chief Tim Love called the trauma command center in Birmingham and told emergency workers there to expect numerous severely injured patients from the fire district. There was no way for him to document these patients, though. There was no time and almost all of the medical forms had blown away in the storm. Two trauma surgeons from the University of Alabama Medical Center arrived to help with triage, and then more rescue workers and volunteers arrived at the disaster scene. Assistant Chief Robbie Miller divided them into groups of five or six and sent them to specific streets to look for wounded residents. At the post, firefighters tried to track as best they could the streets and homes that already had been searched.

Ironically, some of Concord's firefighters would remember a tornado drill the district conducted in Rock Creek in the late 1970s. The mock devastation took up all of a half-acre and the firefighters practiced for the disaster assuming they would have electricity and medical equipment. They figured anything else they needed would be in their fire trucks.

Curtis Poe had been making his way home to Bessemer after working a twenty-four hour shift in Concord when his fire radio squawked to life. "A tornado is on the ground in Oak Grove." Curtis turned his truck around and barreled back over the winding roads to Station One.

Curtis Poe was no stranger to hard times or danger. He was one of the firefighters most respected—if not feared—by the other rescuers. Straight-backed and no-nonsense, he strode into rooms with a confidence that bordered on cocky. He wore round-rimmed glasses but had an Army haircut and a set of muscles that kept him from looking bookish. He had never been a book learner, anyway. He was someone who learned from life.

As a teenager growing up in Adger, Curtis drank a lot, stayed high as much as he could, and skipped school. Marijuana was what he preferred, but when he was seventeen he overdosed on a fistful of pills. His mind hazy and his body almost shut down, he nonetheless remembered a doctor telling his parents that he might not make it through the night. What happened next, Curtis knew he would never forget. His father leaned over him and said, "I want you to go ahead and die, you son of a bitch. I'm tired of you doing this to your mother."

When Curtis lived through the night, he remembered those words. Shamed by his partying past, he stopped getting high and completed Army basic training the summer before his senior year. After he graduated, he trained for four weeks at Fort Benning, Georgia, to become a paratrooper. He learned how to maneuver and to land a parachute. He jumped from a thirty-five-foot tower and then was dropped 250 feet from a helicopter. During his last week of training, he had to make five successful jumps, and when he did, his instructor pinned a pair of wings into the skin above his heart.

Curtis found the purpose he was looking for in the Army. He liked the discipline. He liked being part of something bigger than he was. The Army gave him a future, too. His father had spent most of his working years as a coal miner and Curtis knew that was a job he didn't want. His parents had raised him, his two brothers and his younger sister to be proud of their country; his older brother

Chris also served in the Army and his younger brother Lucky would one day join the Navy. But for Curtis, the Army meant more to him than patriotism. He liked taking charge, carrying a gun, being the one people turned to in a bad situation, being a tough guy.

Once, during a training mission at Fort Bragg, North Carolina, Curtis's parachute didn't open fully. He was not sure he could land safely with the wilted chute. But as he sank lower and lower toward the ground, he realized that if he opened his emergency reserve chute the other soldiers would likely call him a "candy ass," and his Army superiors would make him fill out a lot of paperwork. He couldn't bring himself to reach for the cord. Curtis was the fortieth man to jump out of the airplane that day, and as gravity sucked him down, he soon passed the tenth soldier out of the plane. Still, he left the cord for his reserve chute untouched. He hit the ground hard, was knocked unconscious, and suffered a concussion. A few days later, he was back in the plane ready to hurl himself into the air again. At Fort Bragg, a lot of the men had bumper stickers that said, "It takes more than a badge and a bumper sticker to make a paratrooper," and Curtis believed that.

On the night of the storm, Curtis met firefighter Bobby Hancock at Station One and the two men set out for Rock Creek in one of the district's trucks. Electricity was out all along Warrior River Road and a hard, relentless rain made it impossible to navigate the winding road. Behind the wheel, Curtis cursed. He could see nothing. When they reached 15th Street Road, they had to stop. Upturned trees blocked the road, so Curtis pulled the truck into KC Racing.

Assistant Chief Robbie Miller was there, getting ready to set up a command post. Station Two was gone, Warrior River Road was inaccessible, and there was no equipment to speak of, he told Curtis and Bobby. The number of injuries was bound to be high. Neighboring departments were sending all the equipment and personnel they could. In the meantime, Robbie told the men to get in there and start treating people.

From the back of the fire truck, Curtis grabbed a First Aid box, a tackle box with bandages, IV fluids, blood pressure cuffs, and other supplies, and then he and Bobby headed into the damage. They had no radio and Curtis had no turnout gear. He wore a T-shirt, jeans, and sneakers. The rain had let up a bit, but it was still hard to see anything, except when the lightning sliced up the sky. In those seconds, a harsh, yellow glow, an unnatural light, like the lamps of a homicide squad making day on the scene of a midnight crime, spotlighted piles and piles of trash. It was hard to tell from the debris where one house began and another ended. Nothing had been left whole. Everything was in pieces. People's homes had been emptied of their contents, the sofas, the beds, the clothes in their dressers, the china in their cabinets, and all of it covered the ground, most of it in shards. Walls had been shattered to kindling, and where tall trees once grew, a horizon line now marked the shorn landscape. Sections of roofs lay in the road. At one point, Curtis and Bobby got down on their hands and knees to crawl around a thicket of tree branches. The Army could have dropped Curtis from a plane onto Warrior River Road, and he wouldn't have recognized where he was.

People staggered out onto the main road, limping, holding broken arms, or acting as crutches for injured neighbors. The walking wounded. Soaked and scared, they wore blank looks, the same expressions of horror and confusion that war refugees wore. Curtis and Bobby would let those who could walk on their own go to KC Racing, where a triage station was being set up by the command post. In emergency situations with more than one patient, all rescuers used a system of triage. People suffering from life-threatening injuries—but who had a good chance of survival—received top priority. Rescuers stabilized them or prevented their wounds from worsening or threatening their lives. Then they moved the patient from the hot zone, the disaster scene, to the cool zone, an ambulance or triage site where the person can receive further treatment. Patients with serious, but not life-threatening, injuries were treated next, then patients whose injuries, such as a broken leg, prevented them from moving. Those with cuts or bruises or broken arms were encouraged to walk to a triage station. And those who did not have a chance of surviving were not treated at all.

Glancing around at the bombed-out street, Curtis knew broken arms and fractured ankles would be the most minor of the injuries. There would likely be people who were trapped or buried under the rubble. As he scanned the scene, a teenager wrapped in a blanket—a boy with Down's syndrome—stumbled toward them. In a perfect world, Curtis would have liked to wrap his arms around the scared boy and tell him he was going to be all right. Instead, he flagged down two neighbors and told them to take the kid to the triage station. The firefighters had other people to help.

Back at the command post, Assistant Chief Robbie Miller struggled to bring some control to the situation. Robbie was a quiet man who didn't hang around the other firefighters much. He had a serious demeanor and an accent as thick as sugar on a doughnut. On this night, he had been working at his other job with the Hoover Fire Department when another firefighter told him that Station Two in Rock Creek was gone. His home sat across from the station and both his wife Shelley and his stepdaughter Laura were home. He tried to call Shelley, but there was no answer. His supervisor sent him home.

It took thirty minutes to drive from Hoover to Rock Creek under a heavy curtain of rain, and as he drove, Robbie frantically tried to call Shelley, the neighbor's house, Station Two, anyone who could tell him his wife and their girl were all right. He never got an answer. Finally, five minutes before he reached Rock Creek, a firefighter from Hoover paged him. Shelley and Laura were safe. They had called the station from a neighbor's house. They were alive, but the family's home was destroyed. Once he reached Rock Creek, there was no time for Robbie to find his wife, who was only few blocks away, or to think about his home. He went to work right away, not telling Curtis Poe, Bobby Hancock, or the other firefighters of his agonizing ride into the disaster zone.

One hour after the tornado touched down, meteorologists at the National Weather Service in Birmingham had their eyes on the swirl of a second mesocyclone moving across on the radar screen in a path similar to the storm that had just blown through Jefferson County. Quickly, they issued a second tornado warning for the area.

Rescuers sifting through the first storm's damage heard the news from a Jefferson County Sheriff's deputy, who announced over the radio that another tornado had been spotted and that Oak Grove and Rock Creek could be hit again. This time, no one blew off the storm as just another springtime squall. In Oak Grove, fifteen rescue workers, deputies, and residents crowded into a ten-foot by ten-foot crawl space beneath a store that had been damaged badly. There, they continued to plan the rescue effort as they waited for an all-clear signal.

In Rock Creek, firefighters continued to work as heavy rain fell and thunder boomed around them. Belinda Fitzsimmons, the district's only woman firefighter, was scared, but there was no place for her to go, and there was work to do. "If I'm going to die, at least I am going to die doing something I love," she thought.

After twenty minutes, the downpour stopped. The storm passed without a second funnel cloud. Afterward, a sheriff's deputy stopped a firefighter and asked him if he would convince a woman to come out of her house. The woman wasn't injured and the house still stood. But the deputy felt she should leave. The firefighter was more sympathetic. "As long as she's all right, let her stay there," he said.

In Oak Grove, seven-year-old David Hyche and his younger brother Kyle continued to pray for safety from the tornado's winds long after they died down.

They knew their father, Terry, was caught up in the rescue effort and couldn't stay and help the family, even after a tree had crashed through their house. Their mother, Kathy, led them through the rain to a neighbor's house where they stayed the night. There, they kept up their pleas to God.

"Babies, it's over with. The Lord has protected us," Kathy told them. "We need to just thank Him." Her voice was calm and soothing, like a cool rag on a feverish forehead. But her hands shook as she spoke to them.

David wouldn't let his mother out of his sight. As she settled him and Kyle onto the sofa for the night, he clung to her and begged her not to leave him. She knew he was worried about losing her, that for the first time in his seven short years he knew what it meant to die.

She couldn't think of anything more to tell him, anything that would make him sleep through the night without a worry. Fear gripped her, too. She didn't know why she couldn't make her hands stop shaking. She felt like she was on the verge of a panic attack. Why had this happened, she asked herself over and over again. And why had it happened to them?

Kathy's sister Rachel was still with her and the boys, but she wanted to help the firefighters. She was a nurse and she knew they could use her. The two sisters talked it over in whispers so the boys wouldn't hear them. Kathy was upset and pleaded with Rachel not to go.

"I've got Terry out there already and I can't stand to have you out there, too," she said. She felt selfish for admitting it, but she needed Rachel there. Finally, her sister agreed to stay, and they tried to get some sleep. But every time Kathy closed her eyes she wondered how her husband was doing and what he was seeing out there in the cruel, stormy night.

One story was worse than the next:

The tornado tugged Jim Bradley, a likeable third-grade teacher at Oak Grove School, from his house on Cook Road at the west end of Rock Creek. It hurled him through the air and then dropped him unto a door ripped from a refrigerator. Bones throughout his body were broken and a cut on his scalp would take thirty stitches to repair. Neighbors found the man, wrapped him in a blanket, and sopped up his head with pieces of cloth. They took him out of the rain to a beat-up house that could provide at least a little more shelter. Two hours later, when rescuers finally reached him, he was in and out of consciousness. One of the paramedics remarked that it looked like he had been run through a blender. Bruises covered his body from his waist up, and he had so many broken bones they used a board to splint him, since there was no time to tape each individual fracture. The teacher had been less than a mile from an ambulance, a distance that would take a minute to drive on any clear spring night. He would spend twenty days in the hospital recovering.

Firefighter Belinda Fitzsimmons found five patients—a whole family—at one house not far from 15th Street Road on the east end of Rock Creek. The tornado had lifted the home from its foundation and then dropped it back to the ground, trapping the father. In a neighbor's basement, the man's wife and their three small children tried to stay dry. One of them, a baby, worried Fitzsimmons more than the others. The child could barely breath. Bones in the baby's face were broken and Fitzsimmons could tell that one lung was ruptured, too. She shouted for help and a neighbor ran to her. Fitzsimmons handed her the baby and then started giving the child oxygen from a tank. Lugging the tank, Fitzsimmons guided the woman and the baby over wet boards and broken bricks and out onto Warrior River Road. They tried to run, but couldn't make it very far. Fitzsimmons had to stop every so often to move a piece of metal or a broken branch out of their way. Up by KC Racing, people sat alongside the road with blank stares on their faces and splints on their arms or legs. Fitzsimmons grabbed the gasping baby and handed the child to a doctor. Moving back into the rubble, she had to pause to catch her own breath. She realized she didn't even know if the baby was a boy or a girl.

Firefighter Ronald Waldrop found his cousin Debra's house a mess, pulled apart by the fierce winds and scattered in pieces across the yard. Inside, she and her two small boys had run to the basement where they huddled together as they waited out the storm. But when the house collapsed, a concrete block wall fell on the family. Debra and the boys were killed. When Waldrop found them, he was devastated. His cousin and her boys had done exactly what she was supposed to do by seeking shelter in the basement. But they were dead. It was unfair, wrong even, for children that young to die, he thought. Outside the house, he dropped to his knees and wretched.

As much horror as there was, there were small moments of hope, too:

Dale Byram, who ran the mine rescue team at Jim Walter Resources, the coal company that operated the mines that had employed Concord residents for decades, led a group of five other miners through the maze of trees and broken houses, with their cap lights on their helmets illuminating the way to the injured. It was heartening sight in the black night.

Two of the mine team's patients were an elderly husband and wife. The woman had a broken hip and a stick impaled her husband's leg. Neither one could move, so one of the miners went to retrieve the team's Stokes basket, a rigid, lightweight basket that can be used like a stretcher. The rescuer came back to the house, toting one end of the basket. At the other end was Byram's brother, Kent, a building inspector who lived in Oak Grove. He did not have any rescue training, but he wanted to help.

Kent had a truck with a camper shell that could carry the couple to an ambulance. As the miners loaded the couple into a truck for the triage station, they wondered aloud which one of them would have to leave the group and go with them. If they stuck together, they could search each house more effectively. But a medic needed to stay with the couple. At that moment, a nurse, a woman who lived in the community, stepped up to the men and offered to accompany the injured husband and wife. The rescuers helped her into the truck and waved her off.

Another man—no one ever learned his name—rolled out his own Bobcat and started plowing the road of boards and branches. He cleared paths for several rescuers who said they would never forget his help. But they never found out who he was.

Christie Seals could feel blood filling her lungs, and she called out to her neighbor, Mike Calma. He helped her into a sitting position, and she stayed there as still as she could be. She was scared to turn in either direction for fear that her spine had been broken. She could only see three feet in front of her, but in that bitty space smaller than her oldest boy was tall, she could see nails that had been shot out of boards by the storm's winds. Debris was everywhere. Mike and his wife, Diane, had told her that. It made walking anywhere impossible. But she could hear the two of them now stepping over branches and around piles of bricks and glass. They were looking for John Michael and Margaret. A hard smell of pine, dirty water, and death filled the air. It was an evil smell, an odor that would make her cringe even years later when she remembered it.

For an hour and a half the Calmas searched, until finally Christie heard Mike's voice choke out, "She's OK, Mama." Then Margaret was held in front of her, soaked and crying, and it was like when the doctor who held up her new, little body for inspection after she was born. Tears came in Christie's eyes this time, too. A few minutes later, they found John Michael, also alive. He was not five feet away from his little sister, both of them shielded by a piece of board. Diane took the children to the shelter of a house that partially stood while they waited for rescuers.

Christie kept praying for help. She could hear sirens and she could hear chain saws. They were close, but not close enough. She called out to Matthew and told him that everything was going to be all right, although he still couldn't feel his legs. Her husband wasn't the only one who worried her. Next to her, Nathan jerked in a seizure. His breathing was erratic, and from time to time, it stopped. She talked to him constantly. "People are coming to help us. I love you. Try to hang in there," she told him. She didn't know if he could hear her, but that didn't stop her from trying. The right side of his body leaned into the right side of her body and his head was at her feet. A wet piece of cloth that Mike had salvaged gave them a little warmth, and she hoped Nathan could feel some body heat just from being next to her. It was funny that they had landed at each other's side, she thought. She and Nathan had always been so close. Before Matthew, John Michael, and Margaret had come into their lives, they had only had each other.

"Not even a tornado will separate us now," she thought.

Besides Captain Terry Hyche, there were a few other firefighters who left their own, badly damaged homes and shell-shocked families to help their neighbors. One of them was Richie Miller.

Richie was a big man, with concrete-block shoulders, arms full of muscle, and a shaved head that made him look even more fleshy and brawny. He was the one the other firefighters called on to break down the jammed doors of smoking houses. He saw things simply, which isn't to say that he wasn't emotional or deep. But he thought like a rescue worker. He assessed the situation, did what he could, and then moved on. Already at twenty-eight, his life had collided with disappointment and his stoicism served him well. All through school, he had wanted to play sports. Big and powerful, he had the physique for what he liked best, football, and he played for Hueytown High. He did well on the field until one night when he was out partying with a bunch of guys and got in a car with someone who had drank too much booze to drive. Feeling high himself, Richie wasn't worried. The inevitable car wreck happened on Warrior River Road, between Station One and Station Two. Richie was thrown forty-five feet through the windshield and hit a cement patch headfirst. A helicopter flew him to the University of Alabama Medical Center, where he stayed in a coma for nine days. His jaw had to be wired back together, and one of his only memories of that time was of his father and older brother, Robbie, helping him walk once he regained consciousness. Richie's doctor told him football was out of the question.

So he played baseball. He was good at that, too, and had dreams of winning a junior college scholarship. In his last year of eligibility, a high profile summer league team—the top team of his choice—drafted him. Then two days before the season began, he was on his way to a friend's house when a car ran a stop sign and hit the four-wheeler he was driving. Richie lay in a ditch waiting for the paramedics, his neck broken, his dreams of playing college sports crushed.

He decided to become a firefighter. He had been grateful for the care Concord firefighters gave him after his first accident, and after the second wreck, he decided it was time for him to give something back. He started volunteering with the fire district, where his brother, Robbie, would one day become assistant chief, and then took a job with the Birmingham Fire Department. He had worked for Birmingham for six years as a firefighter and a paramedic and kept a second job as paid district firefighter. He got to be good friends with Chief Love, who stood up as Richie's best man when he got married in 1997. His brother's ex-wife had introduced him to Melanie, who was only twenty-two when they said their vows. She was a petite blond with dark eyes and Richie's second wife. Sometimes, he reckoned, he wasn't really the marrying type, but he really wanted to make things work with Melanie, for the sake of their daughter especially. Christina, "Nina" as he liked to call her, was the one subject that got the big guy to soften. He would do anything for his little Nina.

The Millers lived in a mobile home next to Richie's parents and about a mile from where Robbie lived with his family. The trailer never had a foundation, so the tornado whipped it up easily and dropped it back down close to where it stood. It lurched to one side and dipped down in the middle. To walk from one end to the other would have been like walking up and down a roller coaster track, except that the floor was punched out so nobody really would walk through it anymore. A two by four hung out of the roof. Wet carpet and slivered pieces of furniture hung out of holes like disemboweled innards. A mop that had been drying on the front porch shot out a window in the back of the house. Dirt coated everything and the air held a swampy smell. Behind the house, Richie's two dogs circled their pen, confused. What had they seen?

Richie's parents' home took a heavy hit as well. The winds ripped up part of the roof and then plopped it back on the house. Water filled the garage, and its walls leaned inward. The family's above-ground pool was gone and the wooden deck that surrounded it was broken into pieces, like it had been made of Popsicle sticks.

Melanie covered her mouth and sobbed when she saw the mess of her own home and of her in-laws'.

"At least you're alive," Richie told her. His words came out harshly and he hadn't meant for them to sound that way. He just didn't know what else to say. It was awful and there wasn't anything he could tell her that would change that. And they were lucky the storm hadn't killed them.

From the front yard where he liked to chase around his baby girl, Richie could see storm damage in every direction. One-hundred-year-old trees stripped of their limbs and tossed down like twigs blocked Miller Drive and Old Rock Creek Road. There wasn't one house on his street that hadn't been damaged or demolished. He called Station One in Concord and asked them if anyone had been injured. A firefighter told him there was a patient not too far from Miller Drive who needed his help.

Richie grabbed his fire radio and told Melanie to stay with his folks. "They will look after you," he told her. It was starting to rain and she cradled their baby to her. They had no home. He didn't even now if he had any clothes other than the ones he wore, a T-shirt, a pair of his father's sweatpants, and a pair of his sneakers. But it was his job to treat the injured. Later, he would worry, just like Captain Terry Hyche, that he had deserted Melanie and his little girl.

"Y'all need any help?"

All of a sudden, six or seven big men pushed through the rubble toward Christie Seals. Two hours has passed since the tornado first hit and help was finally there.

"Thank you, God," she whispered. Then she called out to her rescuers, "Yes, we need help."

"How many are in your family?" One of the men was next to her with a flashlight, looking at her leg.

"Five."

"Where are they? Are y'all OK?"

"Nathan's right here with me and he's hurt real bad. He's had a head injury. And Matthew's back there. He has a broken back. The other two children are with the neighbors."

"We'll get your son here first."

They didn't have a stretcher. Instead, Christie watched as they loaded Nathan onto the door from someone's home. Then two of the men took off with her son and another pair came up with a second door for Matthew.

One of the men leaned over Christie again. "Somebody's going to come up and get you real soon, ma'am. We're going to get your little boy and your husband out now. But somebody will be back for you real soon."

"OK." Christie's voice cracked. She didn't want to be separated from Matthew and Nathan. But she knew her husband and her son had to get help as soon as they could. She would have to be left behind. She started praying again for their safekeeping and for the men who had come to save them. It was the only thing she could do to fill the lonely wait.

At what was left of a house at the end of Hancock Drive—a scrap of roof over a foyer—firefighter Richie Miller stood over Nathan Seals, his sturdy, muscled frame a sharp contrast to the little boy's broken, twisted body. A few blocks away stood Richie's destroyed mobile home and his badly shaken wife and little girl. But in the past two hours, he hadn't had one moment to think about them or worry about their safety.

Now he focused on the little boy. Every part of the boy's body struggled as he worked to get air. He seized up, curling up like a baby, and his jaw locked tight. His arms rotated in, while his legs and feet rotated out. He was posturing, a sign that his head injury was severe. His skull wasn't fractured, but the storm had tossed him about so much that his brain had swelled. His pupils were fixed and dilated. Richie shoved a bite stick between Nathan's clenched teeth. "We need to get this boy out," he shouted.

A man who lived nearby had a truck that hadn't been damaged. Lock 17 Road was still shut down, but the man told Richie he could drive Nathan to Rock Creek Church of God. The church was only a block and a half away. That was the farthest they could get by vehicle. Still other rescuers were there and hopefully they could stabilize Nathan. Richie figured one of the trauma helicopters might be up in the air by then, too.

As he helped load Nathan into the man's pickup, another man, a neighbor whose truck also had been spared, pulled up. The man helped Richie load Matthew Seals into the back. Then Richie jumped in with Matthew. As they set off, the firefighter heard a woman shout, "I've still got some good doors if any of you boys need them."

In the truck, Matthew told Richie, "I can't breath. There's something poking me up in my back."

Richie put his hand underneath Matthew but couldn't feel anything. "It's his spine," he thought. "The man's paralyzed." He told Matthew, "I can't feel anything up under there. But don't worry. We're going to get you out of here soon."

They drove through yards and over foundations swept clean by the storm until they reached the church. There, the scene was just as chaotic as everywhere else. But there were other paramedics, Curtis Poe, Belinda Fitzsimmons, and a sheriff's deputy, and they had bandages and IV lines. Richie started an IV on Matthew, while Curtis and the sheriff's deputy looked at Nathan. The boy was still curled into the fetal position and barely breathing. The deputy thought they should wait for a helicopter to fly Nathan to Children's Hospital.

But Curtis wouldn't hear it. "Look, we're taking this little boy and we're going with him," he said.

His voice had the no-nonsense tone of an army sergeant, and it wasn't a bluff. The kid was bad off and Curtis wasn't going to let him die waiting for help. So far, the helicopters had been unable to lift off in the evening's unpredictable and deadly weather, and no one knew when or even if the choppers would arrive. To Curtis, it was simple. Their only choice was to try and make it down the main road to where the ambulances waited on the other side of Rock Creek. It was a gamble, but they had to do something.

By now, the sound of chainsaws sliced through the din around the fire district's main road. Timber and utility crews were sawing through downed trees and sweeping clear one lane of Warrior River Road from the east side of the community. Crews from Alabama Power Company were planting new utility poles and quickly stringing new lines. Curtis thought there was a chance that once the rescuers got as far as where Station Two stood only hours before, or even up to McClain Road, the main road would be passable.

The decision was made. Six rescuers set off, with Curtis and another man carrying Nathan and four other firefighters carrying another patient from the church triage site, a big man who was so cut up he could barely breath. It was treacherous walking. Nothing had been done to clean up the west side of Rock Creek, so the rescuers once again found themselves walking around rooftops, through houses and crawling under trees. Curtis started to wonder if they really could get through to the other side of Rock Creek. But he knew they had to try. The men moved as fast as they could. There were too many landmines in their path to sprint, but their patients were too sick for the rescuers to merely walk.

At one point, the deputy asked, "What do we do if one of them stops breathing?"

"When one of these patients quits moving, we put him down," Curtis told him.

"Even the boy?" the deputy pressed.

"Even the boy."

The man didn't like that answer. Neither did Curtis, really. He would have smacked somebody if they had said the same thing about one of his two little girls. But he knew they had no choice. This wasn't like a car accident where everybody would be bandaged up and taken to the hospital. Some people were going to die before the rescuers even got to them.

"We got to try to do the most good we can for the one that's going to make it," Curtis said in a way that ended the discussion.

Only a few months before, at Christmastime, Curtis had run a call for a house fire in Birmingham that trapped two kids. He and his partner ran out of water and had to dive out a window before they could reach the children, who died in the blaze. Curtis suffered second-degree burns on his face and his partner had second and third degree burns on his back. They wouldn't have minded the burns had they been able to save the kids.

Losing a child reminded him of the worst time in his life, January 1994, when he and his wife, Cassandra, were living in Texas and awaiting the birth of their first daughter. The baby was past due, but wasn't showing any signs of arriving. On the nineteenth, Cassandra called Curtis's sixteen-year-old sister, Brandi, back in Alabama to tell her that, yes, they were still waiting for their little one. Curtis and Cassandra were both close to Brandi. In fact, they had wanted to use her middle name, Leanne, as a middle name for their baby, if she was a girl. But Brandi hated the name and had so strongly argued against it that they relented.

The morning after she talked to Brandi, Cassandra's water broke. When Curtis called his mom to tell them they were at last on their way to the hospital, she sounded upset. Brandi hadn't come home the night before, she said. She wasn't answering her pager either.

All morning and all afternoon, Cassandra labored, and Curtis's family called Brandi's friends to see if any of them knew where she was. Every few hours, Curtis left Cassandra's side to call his mother. Brandi still hadn't come home. In the late afternoon, Cassandra delivered a girl, named Taylor Lynn, just as Brandi wanted it.

That night, Curtis, who wasn't allowed to stay overnight at the hospital, left for paramedic class. Cassandra was nursing their little girl, when a nurse told her she had a phone call. She picked up the phone and heard her husband crying for the first time. He didn't have to say anything else. She knew. Brandi was dead. Police had arrested a boy she knew from school, who later was convicted of raping and beating her and then slitting her throat. Brandi had given him a ride home from school.

Two days after Brandi's body was found, Curtis, Cassandra, and their new baby girl returned to Alabama for her funeral. Curtis worried that Cassandra wasn't up to traveling. But she told him, "You're my husband. My job is to be with you."

Curtis went into combat mode, making sure that Cassandra didn't overexert herself and that his mother had whatever she needed. Everyone else walked around in a daze. Friends brought diapers and baby clothes for little Taylor Lynn. Cassandra collected teddy bears and someone—they never found out whom—brought a baby blanket decorated with bears. She and Curtis felt so strange taking these gifts. They had been blessed with a little girl, but it was hard to be happy. They stayed for a week, but still Curtis didn't want to leave. Back in Texas, he made plans to leave the military and return to Alabama. Once he finished his medical training, he told Cassandra, he would become a paramedic and then they would move back home.

Two years later, he resigned his commission and got a job working for the Birmingham Fire Department. The city's police department offered him a job, too, but Curtis knew that a cop could work for years without drawing his gun. He had never met a firefighter who hadn't been in a burning building. He wanted action. And he got it. He worked in Ensley, on the city's west side, in one of the biggest engine companies in the city. Curtis loved it. Running into a burning house held the same thrill as jumping out of a plane, except that he fought this enemy with a lot more vengeance. If he couldn't beat the crap out of a fire, he took it personally.

Now he felt the same way about this little, gasping boy who was rolled up like an animal ready to die. He knew what he had told the other men had been right: if the boy stopped breathing they would have to put him down and help someone who had a chance of living. But Curtis told himself that the boy would live. "We are going to save this kid, no matter what it takes," he thought.

The men walked for more than a half hour before a man in a pickup, another of the night's good Samaritans, pulled up and asked what he could do to help.

"You think you can get me and this boy up to KC Racing?" Curtis asked. "This boy's hurt real bad and we got to get him to ambulance as fast as we can."

"Yep, I can do that."

In the bed of the truck sat chainsaws and other expensive power tools. Knowing there was not time to unload them, the man jerked his pickup backwards and then forward again, crashing his tools to the ground. He didn't even wince. Instead, he waved to Curtis. "Put 'em right in there, son. Let's go."

Curtis hopped in the bed of the truck and held the boy in his lap. The journey was more of the same. The pickup truck scuttled around tree branches and rain-soaked pieces of furniture. Nathan still wasn't breathing well, so when they met some rescuers from Bessemer, Curtis shouted to the crew for a bag valve mask. He held the child on his lap in the cab of the truck and tried to pump air in the boy's nose and mouth.

"Shit." It didn't work. Curtis didn't have enough room. He stretched Nathan out on the passenger seat and then crouched on the floor to give him air through the mask. "C'mon boy, don't give up." He pumped air into the little boy again and again. "C'mon, we're not that far now."

Finally, the pickup reached the ambulance checkpoint at 15th Street Road. A trauma physician grabbed Nathan from Curtis's arms and began working on him. It had been more than an hour since rescuers pulled the boy from the rubble by his house and more than three hours since the tornado threw him into the night. But they had done it. They had gotten him to an ambulance and now the boy had a chance. Curtis felt sure that Nathan Seals was going to live.

Back on Hancock Drive, race car driver Jimmy Kitchens, his friend Cesar Bustos, and three other volunteers were helping Christie Seals. Although Jimmy's shop was only a mile from her house, Christie had never seen him before. Jimmy was short, extremely fit, with dark brown hair that waved away from his tanned face. He was a charming man, with dreams of NASCAR, who liked to talk about racing, how it was all about the driver's connection with the car moving beneath him. He could make racing sound not like a loud, noisy wild ride, but almost like a sensual experience.

Christie knew nothing about him. She didn't know that he was a race car driver, that he had spent the afternoon testing a car at the Talladega Speedway, or that despite his macho job and convincing smile, his First Aid experience was limited at best. Hell, he had never done much more than put on a Band-Aid, he would admit later. Neither had Cesar, who worked for him. After the day's training at the speedway, they had driven back to KC Racing and heard the tornado warnings over the radio. Like Christie had hours before, Jimmy wondered if it was a false alarm. He had grown up in Alabama, and was used to reports of a little twister. But when they left the interstate, nine miles away from Rock Creek, everything was dark and it stayed that way, all the way to his shop. Nobody had electricity. "This is bad," he told Cesar.

Nothing at KC Racing was damaged. The tornado blew just enough north that it never touched the shop. But a sheriff's deputy told Jimmy and Cesar that the situation was terrible and that they needed all the able-bodied help they could get. He sent the good-looking driver and his friend down Warrior River Road to meet up with Curtis Poe.

Curtis, in his typical no-bullshit kind of way warned them straight out, "You're going to see stuff you've never seen before." Jimmy assured him they could handle it, but since that brief introduction to rescue work he and Cesar had looked for a baby buried beneath a house, had tried to coax a man in shock out of his jeep, and had stepped around at least three dead bodies.

Next, they were sent to help Christie, whose chest now ached as if one of the boards from her house was being driven though it. The men grouped around her and then slowly they eased her onto a straight-back chair that looked like it came from someone's kitchen. The men were kind and gentle, but Christie cried out in pain. It hurt her past words to be handled and moved. A couple of the men apologized. A chain saw rumbled from somewhere close by. Then, one of the rescuers put a board behind her body to support her head, and Jimmy braced her left leg in his hands so it wouldn't be jostled as they skirted the wreckage.

And so they went. For about a mile, the five men carted the injured mother in the straight-back chair, like they were in some kind of bizarre foot race. As much pain as she was in, Christie could see that it wasn't easy for them. Jimmy had to hunch over to support her leg, and at one point, he asked somebody to switch places with him. She felt bad for him.

As the men walked, voices called out to them from the dark houses they passed. There was a man with broken bones who couldn't walk on his own, a woman who couldn't move at all. One by one, men left the group to help these people. Soon Jimmy and Cesar were the only ones carrying Christie. A man who saw the two volunteers struggling to carry her in the straight-back chair offered them his pickup truck. They drove for a little while until they got stuck in the mud. Then, they were back on foot.

Christie felt worse than she had during the whole night. She no longer had the strength to even pray. It was close to midnight. By this time, helicopters spot-lighted the disaster area and bulldozers worked to clear Warrior River Road. Still, a long walk remained before they reached an ambulance.

At last, another bit of luck hit. A couple in a truck offered to drive them to the triage station. It was a bumpy ride and Jimmy and Cesar had to hold tightly to Christie and the chair as they sat in the bed of the truck. Power lines hung so low they nearly touched their heads, and bugs started to swarm through the moist air. The air turned colder. Christie's skin grew clammy and Jimmy started to worry. "Not much farther," he told her.

When they reached the triage site, Christie was laid on a stretcher.

"She needs oxygen. She's turning blue around the mouth." She wondered whom they were talking about. Then a mask came over her nose and mouth.

Jimmy and Cesar stayed with her while a paramedic set her leg. "Who can we call for you?" Jimmy asked. She gave him her sister's number in Atlanta and he promised to call her.

The next morning, on little more than an hour's sleep, Jimmy test drove a car at Talledega, taking it on two-hundred-mile-per-hour laps around the track, whipping around at about the same speed as the tornado's winds.

"Angels come in different forms," Christie told him later.

At Children's Hospital, paramedics pushed the stretcher holding Nathan Seals past the silent waiting room, where on this night nobody's family waited. Instead of holding their babies' hands, parents were being rushed to University of Alabama at Birmingham's trauma center or carried away to the county morgue. Only the beeping and pumping of medical equipment, the quick exchanges of patient information, and the fast movements of nurses and doctors filled the emergency room. There weren't any parents to cry in sadness or in joy. To those who worked there, it didn't feel right.

Nathan was one of twenty-six children who came through the emergency room doors with storm injuries. After he arrived, doctors placed a tube in one of the ventricles of his brain to relieve fluid and pressure. A ventilator in his mouth helped him breath. Another tube through his nose drained his stomach. Six different IVs pumped fluids and medication into his body to, among other things, keep his heart working and to keep his blood pressure regulated. Someone in the emergency room took his picture for identification purposes, and then Nathan was sent to intensive care, the same unit where his mother worked.

Somehow the snapshot made its way to UAB's emergency room. There, Christie Seals held it in her hands. She looked at the little boy with his eyes closed and his hair matted to his head. Tubes surrounded him and there was blood on his pillow. She handed the picture back to a nurse.

"Yes, that's Nathan," she said. "That's my boy." So far, he had made it.

Cold, wet, and sore, the rescuers began to tire from hours of work. Lost with ninety percent of the district's equipment were most pieces of the firefighters' turnout gear. Blood covered their rain-drenched T-shirts and jeans, and pieces of broken homes slit their skin. Their legs and backs ached. The batteries in their handheld radios only lasted a few hours, long enough to supply power during a house fire or a car accident, but not a major tornado. One by one, the rescuers had been cut off from the others. Medical supplies ran short, too. A few workers at a fire station in nearby Bessemer raided a storage locker and dumped everything they could into a pickup truck bound for Concord. In a few hours' time, all of it was gone.

Only months before the tornado, Concord's rescuers had fought the district's first fatal fire in its twenty-four-year history. A young man who lived in Oak Grove caught a couch on fire with his cigarette. He doused the sofa with water and figured he had avoided tragedy. But a fire smoldered in the upholstery and soon the house was full of smoke. The man collapsed a few feet from the front door. His grandmother, who lived with him, died in her bed. Smoke inhalation, the most common killer in fires, got them both.

During a typical year in Concord, car wrecks were the call that district fire-fighters ran the most often, but occasionally a farming accident left someone injured and needing their help. On their rescue truck, the firefighters carried a Hurst tool, backboards, cervical collars, and other tools to force their way any-where. In a half hour's time, they could cut the roof off a car, pull away the dash-board, take out an injured patient, collar him to prevent further injury to the head and neck, and strap him to a backboard. If a passenger wasn't trapped, they could have him in the ambulance, collared, and on a backboard in fifteen min-utes.

On this night, it was four hours after the tornado's touchdown, or shortly before midnight, when the rescuers in Oak Grove finally sent their last patient to the hospital. Three people in that community were dead and a handful had been treated for injuries. Terry Hyche had gone back to his house to get his truck and over the radio in his pickup, he could hear firefighters in Rock Creek still calling for help. "Why are they dragging their feet?" he wondered, assuming that it was Oak Grove that had been hit the worst.

A caravan of rescuers, some in their own pickups and others in engines from Bessemer and Hueytown, and even in one of the beat-up trucks from Station Three, headed east on the winding Lock 17 Road, following a Bobcat whose driver shoved branches and boards to the side of the road. When they reached Auburn Lane, just west of where rescuers had found one man dumped onto a refrigerator door, Terry looked out onto the moonlit landscape and realized that yesterday ten or twelve homes had stood in the emptiness he now saw.

"This is much worse than the damage in Oak Grove," he thought.

For nearly two hours, two crews attacked the disaster zone from both the west and the east side, meeting in the middle of Warrior River Road sometime after two a.m. One hour later, seven hours after the tornado struck, the rescue work in Rock Creek halted. Every wounded person had been transported to the hospital, and there were no more reports of injuries, no more cries in the night. Work crews had cleared one lane's width of Warrior River Road so that traffic could travel from one end of the district to the other. But Chief Tim Love and the other men at the command post decided it would be safer to wait until first day-light to resume an organized house-to-house search for any more bodies.

The rescuers retreated to KC Racing to strategize. Chief Love took a tally of all the workers who were there. In addition to the Concord Fire District, eighteen fire departments were represented. There were countless other off-duty volunteers. One firefighter had driven one hundred miles from Huntsville to help out, even though he knew no one in the area. The sheriff's department had a list of missing persons that rescue workers cross-checked with their reports. By dawn, search crews hit streets. One Concord firefighter served as a guide for each group, since these rescuers knew the area so well. After they searched a house, the crews draped a piece of yellow fire tape around it, so that other rescuers knew the home had been checked. Shortly after seven a.m., firefighter Richie Miller, who had yet to make it home to check on his own damaged house, discovered the body of 83-year-old Verlene Williams buried deep under the debris. Richie had known her all of his life—they went to the same church. Hers was the last body found.

By 8:30 a.m., a little more than twelve hours after the tornado touchdown, rescue workers had finished their search of the entire disaster scene from Oak Grove to Rock Creek. They had sent thirteen residents to the morgue. There were no more bodies to be found and all of the injured had been treated. About eighty percent of the district's five thousand residents could be accounted for. The rest would be found later that day at shelters or with relatives. At last, the rescue work was over.

It was time to tally the damage: As the tornado struck Oak Grove around 8 p.m. on April 8, it took three lives on Griffis Road and then plowed east, to the center of the community where it flattened the fire station and a school. From there, it crossed Lock 17 Road and moved northeast to Rock Creek. At Auburn Lane, it continued to lay waste to every structure in its path. The tornado then crushed houses on Miller Drive, including Richie Miller's mobile home, and smacked into a hillside that overlooked the community. On Dons Drive, fire-fighter Ronald Waldrop lost his house. One street over, on Hancock Drive, it swept the Seals' home from its foundations and claimed five more lives. The greenish-black bank of clouds continued through the heart of the community, destroying the fire station and Assistant Chief Robbie Miller's home. With its path widening, the storm followed Lock 17 Road as it turned into Warrior River Road and five more people lost their lives. Eight minutes after the storm touched down in Oak Grove, the tornado then blew out of the district into several nearby communities, including Sylvan Springs, McDonald Chapel, and Edgewater, and killed eighteen more people. The storm continued through past West Ensley, and in Birmingham's Pratt City neighborhood, historic churches took a beating. But mercifully the storm claimed no more lives.

At 8:30 p.m., the tornado left Jefferson County three miles north of Interstate 20, along Highway 78. In its thirty-mile tirade, the green wind clouds had missed the high rises of downtown Birmingham. Even so, the devastation was staggering. In its wake, the tornado left thirty people dead, one for each mile it traveled, and 252 residents injured. Two others would die of their injuries in the following days. The storm also destroyed close to eleven hundred homes and damaged another one thousand houses and buildings.

All of it happened in half an hour's time.

Part Three: Recovery

o o o o o o o o o o o o o o o o o o o o o o o o o o o o o o o o o o

"When do you consider the recovery part over? I know myself, I haven't felt the same since the tornado. It's affected all of us. We just don't say anything."

—*Firefighter Richie Miller*

In a cold wind, a helicopter landed in a pasture off Warrior River Road and Vice President Al Gore and his wife Tipper stepped out. He looked somber and sympathetic. She wore a sad expression and a fishing vest stuffed with rolls of film. It was two days after the tornado hit.

In his neatly pressed blue uniform shirt and pants, Curtis Poe stood among the ranks of firefighters assigned to the pasture landing site. Secret Service agents told them that if the helicopter crashed, their job was to get the vice president out of the craft. Curtis nodded at the orders, but secretly thought their plan was a joke. If the helicopter crashed, they might not be able to tell which passenger was the vice president and he would grab any body he could. That was his job, not to fish around for someone he could not save. Even if it was the vice president.

It was a bitter morning. No longer halted by the tall trees that used to ring the community, wind whipped into Rock Creek and put a chilly edge on the day. Before the vice president's arrival, the Secret Service and state police shut down every road into the injured communities and set up checkpoints outside of them. As a security measure, none of the residents were allowed into their neighborhoods to pick through the remains of their homes. People parked outside the police barricades and waited impatiently. Concord's firefighters were told that if a fire broke out they would not be able to respond, and one of the district's volunteers was arrested as he tried to make his way into the disaster site. On the radio, a country music station played Elvis Presley singing "Dixie" in a tribute to the tornado's survivors.

At a service station on Warrior River Road, Richie Miller's wife, Melanie, waited. Police shut down the road in front of her. Christina was with her, but Melanie hadn't brought a bottle or any baby food for the quick errands she had wanted to run. She hadn't planned on being away from the house for more than a half hour. But an hour passed. A woman who could see Melanie's predicament took the young mother to her nearby house and they fixed a bottle for Christina. She drove Melanie back to her car, but Warrior River Road remained blocked.

Reporters from CNN, USA Today, and every major television network were some of the few people allowed past the barricades to see the vice president. The storm was a big story for them. Already that year, massive tornadoes had claimed lives in Florida, Minnesota, and Georgia. This was shaping up to be one of the worst spring tornado seasons on record, and it was being blamed on El Niño, the cyclical warming of Pacific Ocean waters that wreaked havoc on weather patterns all over the world. In addition, this latest tornado hit the Bible Belt four days before Easter. In a time for new life and renewal, there was instead death and destruction. Viewers all over the country would soon learn about a church in

McDonald Chapel that collapsed onto a group of nearly seventy worshipers gathered for an Easter prayer meeting. A young church member told reporters how she heard the voices of angels as they strained to hold the pieces of the building off the parishioners. No one was killed.

In Rock Creek, TV photographers stood in the middle of Warrior River Road and turned in a full circle, showing their viewers how the tornado took home after home, chewed them into pieces, and then spit them out in a path of broken boards and split furniture that stretched for miles. Although the road had been cleared of trees and no one was screaming for help, the scene on that April morning was nearly as horrifying as it was two nights before. There was so much damage and the sun put into bright focus every wound and scar. Bits of insulation the size of thumbnails littered the ground and plastered the doors of dented cars. Walls that still stood wore naked strips of wood where the storm sucked away ribbons of paint. Wooded areas looked as if a drunken crew had logged them, and the splintered trees held clothes, pieces of furniture, and shards of metal. Once or twice, shell-shocked residents entered their ravaged homes through the front door, even though none of the walls were left standing. When a teenaged boy who didn't live in the community stopped to talk to an acquaintance who lost her home, the woman politely asked, "How's your mama?" as though he were paying an everyday social visit instead than touring the wreckage of her house.

People seemed to have a hard time believing the scene was real. But it had to have been real, for there were the relief workers handing out First-Aid kits, free tetanus shots, and warm meals in Styrofoam boxes. Police in cars or on foot guarded the streets. Disaster teams made their way through the battered streets to categorize the destruction with red, yellow, or green tags on each house. On certain streets in Rock Creek, every house wore the red tag of total loss.

The churches that still stood became collection sites for the donated clothes and canned goods. A few residents whose homes had withstood the winds rode up and down the streets to offer hammers and hard work to the other families. The grind of chainsaws hummed in the background of media interviews. People pitched tents to guard against looters. Traffic clogged Warrior River and Lock 17 roads. Occasionally, sobs could be heard, and the reporters could smell rain seeping from the wet ruins.

Several reporters wanted to interview Firefighter Scott Swindle, who rode out the tornado inside a rescue truck in Oak Grove's Station Three. Minutes after an off-duty firefighter had telephoned that night to tell him that a tornado was headed for Oak Grove, the wind had picked up and then the tornado siren started bellowing outside the station. As the lights flickered, Scott went into the bay to get a flashlight from the rescue truck, one of three pieces of apparatus parked there. By the time he reached the truck, the power went out. Unfazed, Scott grabbed a flashlight from one of the equipment compartments, a space three feet wide, four feet long, and filled with heart monitors, airway bags, and other tools needed for medical calls or car wrecks. But as he flicked the light on, he heard a roar that filled his ears and blocked out all other sounds. It was the tornado, and that quickly it was there. In the instant it took for Scott to switch on the flashlight, the winds rolled up to the station, and the back wall of the building began to collapse. Scott tossed his fire radio into the truck compartment and then dove in himself. He could not shut the door. Faced in and away from the dangers of the night, he braced his legs against one wall of the metal box and gripped the joints where its sides met. The six-ton truck was his only fortress in the storm, and Scott prayed that he would be safe.

His radio was at his feet, but he couldn't hear the traffic on it. He only could hear the wind's roar, a deadening roar like the noise of jet engines dive bombing toward him, and then the sickening sound of the station's metal siding clanging into the truck. In an instant, the station around him was gone, its siding blown away, its steel frame crumpled. But Scott could not call for help on his radio. If he let go of his grip on the compartment, he feared he would be sucked from the truck. The winds yanked heart monitors and airway bags out of the metal box and he clung to its sides, praying he would not be pulled out, too. Soon the truck started to rock back and forth. Scott panicked. "Please God, don't let it move. Don't let it pick up and go," he begged. He knew he would be killed. Then, just that fast, the winds were gone. Scott got out of the truck and dug out his cell phone to call his wife. The station was gone, but the firefighter was alive.

It was a heck of a story, but not one the firefighter wanted to tell. He turned down every reporter's request and started staying away from the two battered fire stations, in case anyone with a TV camera was looking for him there. His hometown lay in ruins. He didn't even want to think about it, let alone dissect it with a pack of reporters. He also turned down Governor Fob James' request to meet him and he didn't turn out for the vice president's arrival, even though Chief Tim Love urged him to do both.

The vice president gave a press conference in the field where the helicopter landed. Afterward, an assistant pointed out the line of rescue workers guarding the landing site and told Gore that these were some of the same men who saved lives on the night of the storm. The vice president shook each rescuer's hand and told them, "Y'all doing a fine job."

Mrs. Gore followed him, shook every man's hand and then gave each a hug. When she reached Curtis Poe, she put her hands on his waist and leaned in to him. But he didn't return the embrace. Mrs. Gore guessed that the grueling rescue work left Curtis traumatized, and said, "Everybody's forgotten the trauma that y'all must have went through working on this."

"Yes ma'am, it was pretty bad," he said, standing straight and answering as politely as he would have to any of his former Army superiors.

Then the vice president's wife, who had spoken candidly in the past about her own struggle with depression, gave him a sympathetic smile. "You know, you really need to seek professional counseling," she said.

Curtis was not sure what to say. But he remembered his manners and smiled back at her. "Yes ma'am, I probably do," he said. He felt just fine, but it would have been impolite for him to disagree.

Mrs. Gore continued past the paramedic and shook the hand of every rescuer standing in line. When she reached Richie Miller, he offered her his hand and then broke into sobs. Both Richie and his older brother, Robbie, lost their homes in Rock Creek. As news photographers elbowed in to get a picture of the tearful firefighter, he reached over and hugged the vice president's wife.

It was too much emotion for Curtis. "Richie cries and she tells me that I need counseling," he complained later to the other firefighters. He snorted as if to say "hah." What Mrs. Gore said just didn't line up with his way of thinking. The way he figured it, being macho accounted for about seventy percent of his job. He didn't cry, so he was doing just fine. Ain't no way he needed help.

In general, relief workers view tornadoes as one of the most traumatic disasters for a person to recover from, in large part because they occur so suddenly and often with comparatively little warning. People who live next to a rising river, for example, may expect a flood for days before it deluges them.

Tornadoes also appear to be very selective. No one fully understands why some streets will be completely leveled by a funnel cloud, yet residents will find unbroken dishes inside the rubble of their homes. Or why one house will remain standing while the others around it are in ruins. False rumors circulate with the winds; trailer parks draw tornadoes like magnets, or open windows prevent a home from being destroyed.

A storm's unpredictability adds to the increased vulnerability many people feel after a tornado strikes. Survivors can experience nightmares, flashbacks, insomnia, appetite loss, and even guilt for living through the storm. Children may regress to sucking their thumbs or wetting their beds. Parents and children alike can feel clingy and reluctant to be out of each other's sight. People who live through a disaster like this often feel a need to tell their story over and over again. They can become hyper-vigilant about the weather and dread even the smallest rain shower. Other survivors worry that they are losing their minds. The number of suicides in a storm-battered community sometimes rises.

The effects of any disaster can be worse for rescue workers, often because they do not want to admit they are experiencing any post-traumatic stress. After the 1995 bombing of the Alfred Murrah Federal Building in Oklahoma City, for example, some of the firefighters who dug through the wreckage for bodies found themselves turning to alcohol, cheating on their spouses, or considering taking their own lives to forget the pain of what they saw. Their work made them secondary victims to the tragedy. But because they had the wherewithal to handle car wrecks, house fires, and heart attacks day after day, they believed they could handle the trauma from this horrific event. A counselor who worked with some of them in the following years called it "macho-machismoronic," borrowing from the words "machismo" and "moronic." These firefighters tried to be super-human, to let nothing bother them, and if it did, they wouldn't tell anyone even if their pain ate them up inside.

Ted Wilson, who became the Oklahoma City Fire Department's full-time chaplain in the aftermath of the bombing, understood. It was a part of a firefighter's regular job to cowboy up and to keep going through any pain, even after seeing more trauma in two to three weeks than most people saw in their lifetimes. These rescuers were resilient and prided themselves on their strength. They didn't like to talk about their private lives or their feelings, but the chaplain believed they had to before they could put the trauma of the bombing behind them. It left them in an unusual situation, he felt. Their communities relied on them to be tough enough to run into desperate situations, the burning homes or bombed-out buildings that everyone else ran out of. Yet, rescue workers had to be sensitive enough to realize when these disasters affected them personally. If they didn't, it could tear up their lives.

On Easter Sunday, Curtis Poe was working on his regular shift with the Birmingham Fire Department when he transported a child to Children's Hospital, the same medical center where Nathan Seals had been taken in the hours after the tornado. After his patient was admitted to the emergency room, Curtis went upstairs to the critical care unit to see Nathan. It was something he never did, check up on a patient he had treated. Few rescuers did for fear of becoming too emotionally involved. But Curtis had become attached to the little boy that night. He really wanted to see him, to know that he was all right.

On the unit, Curtis explained to a nurse that he was one of the paramedics who had worked on Nathan in the hours after the storm and that he would like to visit with the young boy.

The nurse quietly said, "He just passed away. His family's in there with him."

"Oh." Curtis felt like the wind had been kicked out of him. He shook his head. It was unbelievable. Nathan was dead. He wasn't supposed to die. Curtis had carried him through broken homes and battered streets. Sure, there were times that night he wasn't sure the boy would make it through the journey. But when he did, Curtis took it as a sign that Nathan was going to live. He would recover and grow up, and the storm would just be a faint memory in his mind, something that might make him jump when lightning flashed outside. Nathan wouldn't die now. Not after all that Curtis and the others went through to save him. No, that just wasn't right.

"Did you want to pay your respects to the family?" the nurse interrupted his thoughts.

"No," he said. He was angry and he didn't want to face a weeping family. Quickly, he turned around and left the hospital.

The numbers had been calculated. Of the eleven pieces of fire apparatus the district owned, only the three at the untouched Station One in Concord weathered the storm. Eight other pieces of equipment had to be repaired or replaced. Ninety percent of their equipment was gone. To replace only one engine and all of its lost equipment would cost the Concord Fire District $40,000. To replace everything would cost $1.4 million. It was staggering to think about.

So much was needed. First there were the hoses—fifteen hundred feet of five-inch hose, four hundred feet of one and three-quarters inch hose, two hundred feet of one-inch booster hose—all of which were used to fight different types of fires. Then there were the adapters to connect all these lines of hose, the nozzles with pistol grips, the couplings, and the wrenches to take apart the hoses once a fire was out.

Of course, there was other equipment, too. Ladders, handheld lights, fans to blow smoke out of a building, and special tools to fix the district's fire hydrants, which were a model no longer made. Every firefighter had to have turnout gear as well, the fireproof jacket, pants, and boots that kept them safe. They needed helmets and air packs, or tanks of air that let them breathe inside a smoke-filled building. This equipment was the bare bones of what they needed. There had been no fancy stereo systems or drink warmers in the fire engines, no luxury items in their toolboxes.

Firefighters from other departments lent workers and equipment, and even sent off-duty firefighters to patch roofs and make home repairs for the Concord men who could not leave their posts. Both Bessemer and Hoover fire departments lent fire engines to the beleaguered district. All of this generosity was heartening, particularly since rivalries had flourished between Concord and a few of its neighbors in the past. Still, the district could use borrowed trucks for only so long. There were other problems, too. Nearly every paid district firefighter worked long hours in the days after the disaster, and there wasn't enough overtime pay in the budget to cover the costs. People needed to go home, but there was so much work to do.

Then Chief Tim Love discovered an even greater problem. Years before, when the district was under different leadership, insurance coverage had been cut as a way to stay within the annual budget. While the district's loss was calculated at $1.4 million, its insurance only covered $375,000 worth of damage. Within a few days of the storm, the insurance company delivered a check for $330,000 with a promise for the remaining $45,000. But that still left the district short of more than $1 million. No one knew where it would get the rest of the money.

Even worse, Chief Love learned that the lease on the land they rented from the county school board for Station Three in Oak Grove had expired two years before the storm. That meant that even if the firefighters found the money to rebuild their Oak Grove station, they had no place to put it.

Even on the best of days, the life of a part-time, rural fire chief was hardly a glamorous one. Quite often, it meant handling the situations that no one else did. Once when a firefighter slept through a midnight call for a sick woman, it took fifteen minutes for a man from the next station to reach her. That was about ten minutes too long for the woman's daughter, who complained to the chief. He promised her it wouldn't happen again. A few weeks later, his radio toned out a second late-night call to the mother's address. She was sick again. Chief Love listened to the message from his own bed. The same sleepy firefighter was on duty that night and the chief waited to see how long it would take the rescuer to get moving. A minute passed. Then another one. Chief Love cursed, rolled out of bed, and grabbed some jeans. He raced to the scene in his own truck, arriving at the same time as the firefighter who was backup for their slowpoke co-worker. This time, Chief Love made sure the family had nothing to complain about.

At thirty-five, Chief Love was a young commander with boyish energy. He kept his graying hair clipped short and had the skinny physique of someone who could put away a lot of meat and potatoes at lunch, but couldn't sit still for the rest of the afternoon. Out of high school, he had worked as a mechanic and then started volunteer firefighting on the side. At first, he didn't think he'd like rescue work enough to overlook the blood and guts of the job. He was wrong. Like so many emergency workers, he got hooked by the adrenaline rush almost as soon as he got started. Later he took a full-time position with the Birmingham Fire Department, a job he kept after he became Concord's chief. In many ways, he was a good leader. He was friendly, a good talker—especially when the subject of hunting came up—and often a fair judge of people. He was full of motivation, but also was one of the guys. Generally, the chief liked to look at the bright side of things, but after the tornado he took up smoking again.

At Station One, he called several emergency meetings to discuss the district's predicament. Rescuers jammed the phone lines with calls to equipment manufacturers, and volunteers dropped off meals for the weary workers. Teams of rescuers revved up their own pickups to pull pieces of debris and steel poles from where Stations Two and Three had stood. A businessman who heard about the losses donated a Winnebago for the firefighters to use as their Oak Grove station. Later, they replaced the camper with a rented trailer, and two tarpaulins that were rounded like Connestoga wagons protected the engines parked outside. Station Two was closed indefinitely.

Then, on the last day of the Alabama State Legislature's thirty-day session, lawmakers passed a resolution that provided money for a new Oak Grove School and gave the Concord Fire District $740,000 to rebuild their fire stations. Now the firefighters would have nearly all they needed to rebuild. In addition, they soon learned that the Federal Emergency Management Agency would cover all the overtime costs from the rescue effort and cleanup. Chief Love shouted for joy. They had come so close to closing their doors for good in two communities. But once they bought a new piece of land for Station Three, the two stations lost to the storm could be rebuilt. It felt like a miracle.

In the days after the storm, the city's trauma network, Birmingham Regional Emergency Medical Services, held a special support group meeting for emergency workers who wanted to talk through their feelings in the aftermath of the tornado. A BREMS representative invited the Concord firefighters. But with all their money worries, their lost equipment, and their damaged homes, none of them could spare an hour or so to talk about their feelings. One rescuer told BREMS that it was too early to go through a stress debriefing, that he wasn't through getting stressed yet. "You know, we got work to do here," he said. "We'll worry about debriefing and getting rid of the stress when the stress is over."

On the morning after the disaster, meteorologist Brian Peters hovered in a state police helicopter over the tornado's path. From up in the sky, there was no mistaking the thirty-mile-long war zone that stretched from Oak Grove to Rock Creek, where fourteen people had died, to Sylvan Springs and then to Edgewater and McDonalds Chapel, where fourteen more people lost their lives. Street after street of homes had been erased in a long line of devastation that stretched to Pratt City, a predominantly African American community inside the western edge of Birmingham. In addition, a second tornado from the same storm system had caused damage in Pickens and Tuscaloosa counties, and a third twister had touched down in St. Clair County, where it claimed two lives. The giant storm system that spun out these tornadoes then traveled through Calhoun and Cleburne counties before it finally crossed the Georgia line, where twisters destroyed hundreds of homes and killed two more people. By the end of the day on April 8, dozens of communities had been affected by this system, and the National Weather Service had issued 109 storm warnings.

From his seat in the sky, Peters calculated that the deadliest tornado of this trio, the storm that pummeled the Concord Fire District, measured a massive three-quarters of a mile at its widest, which was as it left Rock Creek and moved eastward. On the ground, Peters walked past mangled cars and foundations wiped clean as he snapped photos and studied tree trunks. From the damage, Peters calculated the tornado initially had winds from 158 to 206 miles an hour as it touched the ground and passed through Oak Grove. It was strong enough to destroy metal or masonry structures, which made it an F-3 on the Fujita-Pearson scale.

The F-scale, as it was known, was devised by late meteorology professor Theodore Fujita and, after it was adopted by the National Weather Service in 1973, became the most commonly used gauge for a tornado's strength. The F-scale ranked a tornado's power by the destruction it left behind, from F-0, the weakest of tornadoes, to F-5, the strongest. The difference could be tremendous. An F-0 broke branches off trees, damaged chimneys or TV antennas, and shattered some windows. An F-5 storm lifted strong frame houses off their foundations, debarked trees, spun cars through the air, and badly damaged even steel-reinforced, concrete structures. Wind speeds associated with an F-0 storm were believed to be from 40 to 72 miles per hour. The winds associated with an F-5 storm were from 261 to 318 miles per hour.

From what Brian Peters could see, the April 8 storm caused little damage as it began its life on the ground, but then quickly became an F-3 tornado with winds of less than two hundred miles an hour. It started chewing up houses and razing trees, and as the funnel cloud moved from Oak Grove to Rock Creek, it caused considerably more damage. That could be explained, in part, by the larger number of Rock Creek homes in the storm's path. But the tornado also grew stronger after it left Oak Grove, Peters figured. As it moved down Warrior River Road, there was evidence that its frenzied winds spun at a speed greater than 260 miles per hour, the speed of an F-5 tornado.

At the time of the Alabama disaster, only one percent of tornadoes grew to be powerful F-5 storms. But these tornadoes always blew their way into the evening news. In 1997, an F-5 tornado wiped out an entire subdivision and claimed twenty-nine lives in and around Jarrell, Texas. The tornado was one of six spawned by a line of violent thunderstorms that pummeled central Texas on a late May afternoon. The tornado's ferocious winds pulled grass from the ground, spiraled more than a dozen cars through the air for more than a mile, and killed 300 head of cattle, according to a National Weather Service report.

Overall, fifty F-5 tornadoes struck the United States between 1950 and 1998. Texas, Kansas, Iowa, and Oklahoma, four states in the country's infamous Tornado Alley, weathered the highest number of these storms. But F-5 tornadoes also hit Alabama four times—once during the Super Outbreak of 1974 and then three times on one violent day in 1977 when a trio of F-5 tornadoes shook Guin, Tanner, and Mt. Hope. All four of these storms struck the state in the first few days of April. Eight days after the tornado that hit the Concord Fire District in 1998, another funnel cloud touched down near Waynesboro, Tennessee, close to the Alabama state line, and killed three people. The National Weather Service also rated that tornado as an F-5, although other reports differed.

For Brian Peters, it was chilling to walk through the destruction from a tornado he had watched develop on the radar screen the day before. Face-to-face with the ruin the storm left behind, he thought how vulnerable people were to nature's power. That frustrated him. Even though meteorologists had seen this storm coming and provided ample warning time for residents in the affected areas, scientists still had a long way to go before they would be able to specifically detail the magnitude of an approaching tornado. In other words, they would not know until it was over how bad a storm was.

Two days after the tornado hit and one day after Brian Peters' data gathering, a three-man team from Texas Tech University's Wind Engineering Research Center began another investigation of the damage. For three days, they studied evidence in a seventeen-mile swath of the storm's path. They started by watching a tape of the affected area filmed by members of the Alabama National Guard. Then they began their tour. The first stop: the Concord Fire District.

The team, which consisted of Russell Carter, a research associate, James Snelson, a graduate student in mechanical engineering, and Gary Skwira, a graduate student in atmospheric sciences, documented how roofs came off homes and how walls collapsed. They studied houses that withstood the storm and those that didn't, taking pictures of much of what they saw. They also examined missiles, or pieces of debris picked up by the storm's winds and dangerously catapulted into homes or other structures. Missiles can be boards or tree branches broken loose in the winds. In more powerful storms, cars become missiles chucked like darts. In some cases, missile damage can have as much impact as a tornado's gusts.

The team approached their work like it was a forensic science, working backwards from the pieces of debris until they could determine how a structure came apart. Carter was a veteran of powerful storms. In 1997, he toured the damage after the deadly tornadoes in Arkadelphia, Arkansas, and Jarrell, Texas, and in 1998, he also visited tornado-ravaged central Florida and Spencer, South Dakota. But he found himself amazed by the disaster scene in Alabama and described it as some of the most severe damage he had ever seen.

To determine the storm's wind speeds, wind researchers examined homes that were destroyed to learn at what wind speed they would fall apart in a storm. That number was estimated to be the storm's lowest wind speed. Then, researchers looked at structures that still stood and considered the speed of winds necessary to have destroyed them. That storm's highest wind speed was estimated to be less than that number.

On Rock Creek Road, between the Concord Fire District and the community of Silvan Springs, Texas Tech's team found something curious. Three homes not more than two hundred yards apart had sustained dramatically different damage. One two-story home, built at least twenty years before, had been uplifted by the storm's winds and deposited upside down in a ravine. The second home had been built less than five years before the storm and had a reinforced-concrete, walkout basement. The storm stripped the metal siding off the home's roof and broke several windows, but caused little more damage than that. The third home had a concrete-block basement. But it was not reinforced, so the blocks were not bound together by concrete or steel. When the tornado's winds hit, the home slid apart like a tower of toy blocks as its masonry broke at the joints.

These houses were close together, so the wind speeds that affected each one were likely the same. They were high—there was no doubt in Carter's mind the wind blew at more than one hundred miles per hour. But winds from 110 to 160 miles per hour could have caused the damage to these three homes. Carter was aware that studies of most major tornadoes since 1970 revealed that a majority of buildings failed or were destroyed in winds of less than two hundred miles per hour. He and the other two Texas Tech researchers eventually reached the same conclusion as the National Weather Service: The destruction left in the wake of this storm was consistent with damage caused by an F-5 tornado. But in contrast to the Weather Service, they believed that the tornado's winds never topped 160 miles per hour. They were a few of the many researchers, who at the time of this tornado, believed that the wind speeds assigned to the Fujita scale categories were too high. Not everyone would agree with the assertion, and even those who did would argue that the F-scale remained the best instrument they had to gauge the severity of a storm. It was a debate without quick resolution and, while perfecting the science was important, neither viewpoint provided much shelter for families cowering in their homes as the black clouds of a supercell spun closer. Either Mother Nature could whip up winds of 260 miles per hour, or a tornado did not have to be as strong as scientists once thought to tear apart homes and communities like the storm in Alabama did on the night of April 8.

There had been a misunderstanding that Curtis Poe would not know about for more than a year after the trauma of going to see Nathan Seals in the hospital: Nathan was close to death on the day Curtis had gone to see him, but did not die then. That morning, doctors worried they would lose him, so they sent for his mother Christie who came by ambulance from UAB where doctors were continuing to treat her chest injuries and broken leg. Matthew, who was paralyzed, as everyone had feared, could not be released. Christie spent three hours at Nathan's side and was there when Curtis came to see her son. The two never met. She left physically exhausted, but relieved. Her son was still alive.

All night, she waited with dread to be told that he had died. She dreamt that he was standing in front of her with his arms at his side and his mouth shut. But she could hear his voice and he told her he was going to be all right. The next morning, she found out that Nathan was still alive. He was in a coma and his chances of living through it were very small. Still, Christie and Matthew would not let doctors remove his life support. They could not pull away whatever chance, however thin, that he had.

After a few days, however, Christie could see that Nathan was not getting any better. Drugs pumped into his body sedated him and left him immobile so that he wouldn't fight against the breathing tube and the other equipment attached to him. With his body basically shut down, all he had to do was heal and mend. The swelling in his brain went down, the fluid in his lungs drained. But his kidneys stopped working. He was hooked up to a dialysis machine at his bedside, but there was a risk that it would trigger more bleeding in his brain. His body was stiff, his limbs hard, his feet pointed down. The dialysis machine pumped the sedation drugs from his system. If he were going to wake up, it would have happened once the drugs drained from his body. His eyes stayed closed. For eight hours and then twelve hours and then a whole day. Christie's family told her not to give up hope. But her years as nurse told her differently. She knew he wasn't going to wake up. Nathan's heart rate was stable, and then it dropped. The bleeding in his brain got worse. No one had to explain it to Christie. She could read the chart and see his prognosis. She looked at her son and knew. Ten days after the tornado hit, Nathan died.

Years before, when he was just three or four, Nathan had told his mother that he wanted to go to heaven. In fact, he wanted to go when he was five. He told Christie, "When I am five, I'm going to go to heaven," just like that, like some children tell their parents, "For my sixth birthday, I want to go to Disney World." Nathan knew about heaven and the afterlife from Sunday school, and heaven seemed like wonderful place to him, because he could climb trees there and swim in the River of Life.

Christie told herself his words were just child's play, but she asked God to let her have her son as long she could. When he turned six without any tragedy, she relaxed the grip her heart held on him. Her baby was safe. He would be hers forever. A blind spot grew. She didn't tell him not to run in the street, to be extra careful when he climbed a tree. Then, two years later, he was gone. When Christie told her son goodbye, she said, "You go climb the trees and swim in the River of Life. I'll catch up with you."

Scars from the storm blighted Concord's two devastated communities for months and told the tornado's story to anyone driving through town. In Rock Creek, a set of brick steps that once led to Hazel and John Allison Brown's home dropped off into nothing. The tornado collapsed the home, killing the Browns. Somehow no one could bear the task of tearing down the steps or the bushes that had became the tallest greenery left in the windswept yard.

Firefighter Richie Miller had no hard feelings about hauling away the remnants of his mobile home. The sooner that heap was gone, the sooner he and his wife Melanie could get a new mobile home. From their battered house, they were able to salvage more than they had hoped, a sofa, some photographs, clothes, and pots and pans. They even found a pair of Melanie's porcelain angels untouched on a damaged shelf. They planned to put their new home in the same place as their old one, on the bit of land they owned in Rock Creek next to his parents' place. Despite the storm, they weren't ready to abandon Rock Creek.

After the Millers' house was destroyed, Melanie and Christina went to live with her mother in another Birmingham suburb. Richie borrowed a rollaway bed from the Concord Baptist Church and moved into Station One. For nearly three months, he lived there, pitching in with the fire district's rebuilding efforts, handling his family's insurance claim, and reporting for duty at his firefighting jobs in Concord and Birmingham. He couldn't stand to be away from Melanie and Christina, and visited them once a week. But as the family provider, he felt it was up to him to get his wife and daughter a new home to live in so they could be together again as soon as possible. That was the only way they could get on with their lives. He spent every spare minute planning for his family's return to Rock Creek.

The Millers' old mobile home never had a foundation. It rested only on its wheels and axels, which Richie believed helped cushion the blow when the storm winds dropped it back to the ground. But he didn't want their second mobile home to be able to even leave the ground. Fourteen steel tie-downs anchored the new double wide into the ground and then a concrete foundation was poured around them. The Millers bought new bedroom furniture and a new kitchen table and moved into their home two months after the storm.

It was beautiful. The rose carpet smelled fresh, and everything gleamed like it should in a new house. Richie was so proud. He had lived in the old home with his first wife and he knew that bothered Melanie a little. For the first time, they would have a home they had chosen together.

As other families scrambled to rebuild, one landmark that remained missing from the landscape was the Oak Grove School. For more than a century, the school stood watch over an area that grew up around it. Generations of the same family attended classes there. Husbands met their wives there. At the time of the tornado, about twelve hundred students, ages five to seventeen, attended the school. Its graduates and students missed the old place and its familiar façade on Lock 17 Road. Every time residents drove by, the empty landscape reminded them of what was not there. The face of their community was gone.

Admittedly, it had not been a pretty face. Necessity, not planning, dictated the school's construction over the years as new buildings replaced older, dilapidated ones. The result was a hodgepodge of a few structures that included cramped classrooms and a cafeteria shared by kindergartners and high schoolers alike. Then there was the school's history with storms. Twice before the April 8 storm, fierce winds spun through the property and damaged the buildings, once in the 1950s and then again in the late 1960s. Both storms, believed to have been tornadoes, left little damage. Yet in a community that strongly believed disaster could not strike twice, here was a school that storms battered more than once and then pummeled into nothing decades later. Graduates who held fond memories for the well-worn place did not bring up this point too often. Hours before the tornado, kids sat in classrooms, waiting for the final bell in what had been an average school day. That night, many of them lost their homes. But one of the few blessings of the storm, people would say later, was that the tornado struck when it did. If it had hit Oak Grove in the afternoon, many of Concord's rescuers believed that dozens of school children would have died. Parents shuddered at the thought when they drove through Oak Grove and found their eyes scanning the valley for the missing buildings.

After the storm, people gathered up the building's bricks like souvenirs. They seemed even more important to keep than old yearbooks or varsity letters. Meanwhile, the school system bused the elementary and middle school students twenty-one miles away to trailers at McAdory High School for the remainder of the school year. The high school students attended classes in trailers at Gilmore-Bell Vocational High School in Hueytown, sixteen miles from Oak Grove. But the seniors who would have spent their last days at the Oak Grove School collected their diplomas in a graduation ceremony on the school's baseball field.

As summer stretched ahead, students and parents waited for word on a new school. Everyone assumed it would be built in the same location as the old one. After all, the school had been in Oak Grove longer than any other building. But as the wait continued rumors spread: the school would be shut down and from then on the children would be bused to other communities. There was evidence to support the gossip. Parents learned that the twenty-eight-acre school property was not large enough for a new school. A state law passed long after the Oak Grove School opened its doors required a new school of its size to be built on at least forty-five acres. Meanwhile, the fire district was supposed to be receiving money from the state to rebuild their Oak Grove station, which had been on land leased from the school board. But construction on the station had not started. People wondered if neither the school nor the fire station would be rebuilt. Word got out that the school property rested on deep coal deposits. The site bordered property owned by U.S. Steel Corporation's mining division. If the steel company, which at one time had been the Birmingham area's largest industry, wanted the land, parents felt sure that they would get it. That could put an end to plans for a new Oak Grove School and probably a new fire station. Alarm spread.

Then, the school board made an announcement. There would be a new school in Oak Grove. As it turned out, U.S. Steel was interested in the old school property, so much so that the company traded eighty-eight acres for the school's paltry twenty-eight. Two new buildings—an elementary and middle school and a separate high school—would be constructed about a mile and a half from the old site. The high school would have two gymnasiums and a full auditorium with a stage for community theater productions. There would be football, baseball, and softball fields. The elementary school would have its own media center for the first time. Both schools would have their own cafeterias. The buildings were scheduled to be completed by August 2000 and architects started planning immediately for the construction. In addition, the fire district would receive a plot of land east of the old station, but still in the heart of Oak Grove. There would be a new station, more than twice the size of the old one, open by January 1.

The news about the school earned mixed reviews. The community would have its landmark again. That was reason to celebrate. But many mourned the fact that the new buildings would not stand where the old school presided over the community only months before. That would change Oak Grove forever.

"I don't want to go back to school," seven-year-old David Hyche told his parents.

After the storm hit, David got a crash course in weather and safety, and he knew a mobile home or a trailer wasn't a safe place to be when cyclone winds blew. But until the new Oak Grove School was built, a trailer at McAdory High School would be his classroom. All of his classmates would be bused there. It worried David, a serious boy with dark eyes like his mother's and a keen awareness of the storm's effects. Their house didn't have a cellar, so when bad weather threatened David liked to go to his grandmother's house and stay in her basement. Even if the weather was moderately windy, he called his father at work and asked him to come home. The boy could read weather maps as well as any adult, and sometimes even spent days tracking bad weather moving into the Southeast from as far as Texas. Every time thunder clapped, he turned on the TV.

"Everything's going to be just fine," Kathy tried to comfort her son. But secretly she and Terry worried about their little boy's preoccupation with weather. Before the storm, David had been such an optimistic kid. There wasn't anything he didn't think he could do, and he liked to do whatever his father did. Mainly, the two liked to fish together and David could stay out all day on the water without a complaint. He was conscientious, too. Terry could trust him to stay away from the power tools a kid shouldn't touch, while he had to keep a watchful eye on David's younger brother, Kyle. Both boys were just average kids who played T-ball and spent their summer days riding bikes. But while Kyle seemed to take the storm in stride—his parents figured he was too young to understand all that happened—the tornado changed David.

That night, before disaster struck, Terry had reassured David that the tornado would never hit Oak Grove. He figured a tornado had not hit the community in recent years, so the community would be spared from this storm. It felt safe to think that way. Disasters didn't happen in the Concord Fire District. They happened on TV, in faraway places, to people they didn't know well enough to wave to in the grocery store parking lot. But he was proven wrong. Afterward, his Concord coworkers liked to tease him about it and he sometimes joked about his bad prediction himself. But he could not get beyond the feeling that he had let his son down by telling him the family was safe from tornadoes, when in fact the storm was seconds away from battering their house. What was worse was that David had asked Terry a few days after the storm why he had had to leave that night, why he had to go help so many other people when his own boys and his wife had to fend for themselves.

"Because that's my job," Terry told his son. That was what rescue workers did. They put aside their own lives to help people in need. It was the best answer Terry could give David. But he knew in his heart it wasn't enough. Minutes after the most horrific event in his family's life, he told his wife and sons he couldn't stay and take care of them, and then he walked out the door. He chose the community over his own family. It was what he had to do, but it meant that he had let down the three people he loved most.

Both Terry and Kathy grew up the children of Baptist ministers, and family was a strong force in their lives. The couple met in the early 1980s through a church youth group. Kathy was fifteen and Terry was nineteen. Three years later, after Kathy turned eighteen, they married. By the time the tornado hit, they had been together for more than half of Kathy's life and had been married for fourteen years. Both of them remained devoted to religion. They often prayed together as a family, and neither of them believed in drinking or smoking. Their one vice, Kathy sometimes joked, was that they were both overweight.

After the tornado, Terry had little time for either his family or the church. There was so much work to do to bring the fire district back to where it had been before the storm, and Terry felt like he was playing catch-up from day to day. Often, he told his minister he would be there for Sunday services. But often he was not. Terry hated that fact. He felt like he was thrust in a fast lane of traffic on the night of the storm and had not slowed down since. It reminded him of a trip to the mountains that he and Kathy took before their two boys were born. During their first day there, both of them—accustomed to the fast pace of life at home—rushed through their meals until it suddenly dawned on them that they were on vacation. They could slow down.

Sometimes Terry talked with the other men at the station about his fears of letting down his family. But he didn't share any of these feelings with Kathy. In fact, they rarely mentioned the tornado. She heard other firefighters talk about finding bodies, but her husband never spoke about any of this with her. As their son continued to worry about the weather, she began to wonder if Terry was trying to shelter her and the boys by not talking about the storm. Kathy didn't want to be protected. She wanted to hear about what Terry had seen. She wanted to hold him and tell him it would be all right. She also wanted to protect her boys. The more David worried about storms, the more she realized she too could not stand the thought of them being in a trailer either. She took David and Kyle out of school and decided to homeschool them herself. "Once the fire stations are rebuilt and once Terry has more time for our family, everything will be back to normal," she thought.

On May 9, one month and one day after the disaster, meteorologists at the National Weather Service in Birmingham noticed a strong pattern of red and green on Doppler radar that looked suspiciously like the mesocyclone that spawned the April 8 tornado. It had a similar structure and similar rotation speed. It even threatened the same area of western Jefferson County at the same time of night. Storm spotters in Concord and Pleasant Grove reported hail at 7:41 p.m. on May 9, just two minutes before the time meteorologists had issued a tornado warning for Jefferson County on that fateful April day. Immediately, the weather service issued tornado warnings. The unthinkable was happening again.

Storm spotter Eddie Maxwell kept watch on the same hillside where he saw the April tornado close in on Rock Creek. To him, it was the replay of a nightmare. Not only did the storm's radar pattern have a close resemblance to the April 8 tornado, its thick, solid clouds looked almost identical to Eddie as he watched them move into Jefferson County. Strobe-like lightning lit up the sky and hail fell. As Eddie picked up his ham radio receiver to describe what he saw, he wondered if the people listening to his report would really believe it. Everything he detailed was exactly what he had described on April 8. Would someone think he was playing some kind of sick joke?

Back in Rock Creek, no one second-guessed the radio reports. No one wanted to take a chance against nature this time. People ran for cover like they were running for their lives. A young girl who lived next door to the Maxwells sprinted so fast for their basement that she fell and broke her arm in two places.

In nearby Bessemer, Terry Hyche was working that night on his regular shift for American Medical Response ambulance service when Kathy called with a voice full of worry. The tornado warning had upset David and he wanted to talk with his father. The child sobbed into the phone and nothing Terry said would calm him. Finally, he went home to console his son.

Tense moments passed as people in basements prayed for the all-clear signal. They remembered the roaring sound of jets and the bomb-like explosions of foundations being wiped clean. The air felt heavy with humidity, like it had a month before, and thunder boomed around their houses. On TV, there were reports from storm spotters who saw a funnel cloud. But no one reported any tornado damage. This time Jefferson County was spared.

Months later, meteorologist Brian Peters would compare the radar images from the two storms and would swear they were the same. Scientists could not say why one supercell developed into an F-5 tornado and the other did not. People told themselves that lightning did not strike the same place twice. They had lost so much the previous month. This time, they deserved to be spared.

Then, several weeks after the May 9 scare, another storm hit, this time with fierce straight-line winds. Curtis Poe and Scott Swindle were working that night in Oak Grove. Sitting outside the trailer that served as Station Three, they watched black storm clouds sweep in over a field behind the fire trucks. The clouds kept moving closer and the two men realized they were about to be hit by a big storm. They clamored into the safest place they could, into the cab of one of the fire engines.

"Here it goes all over again," Scott thought. He could not believe his bad luck. Overhead, the storm clouds moaned and cracked open to a downpour of rain. Scott listened for, but did not hear, the sound of a tornado, the mighty roar that he swore he would never forget. Still, he felt like he and Curtis were about to be rattled around by something powerful. He knelt on the floor by the passenger seat and prayed out loud, "Please God, not again."

Curtis, who had donned a tough guy exterior ever since Nathan Seals died, refused to be frightened. Instead, he started laughing and teasing Scott. "This is worth it just to see you on your knees praying," Curtis told him.

Almost as quickly as the storm blew in, it blew out again. Despite its heavy rains and fierce winds, neither man was injured. But the strong gusts ripped up a canopy that was the only roof over Station Three's two engines, and it dented the cab of Engine Three, one of the vehicles damaged in the tornado and repaired later. Lightning wasn't supposed to strike the same place twice, but apparently windstorms could.

For many communities across the nation, the spring of 1998 was a deadly and destructive season. Eighty-one percent of the 129 people killed by tornadoes that year lost their lives before June 1.

The Southeast weathered the majority of the year's vicious storms. While violent weather for the most part spared Tornado Alley, Florida, Georgia, Alabama, and Tennessee all faced fierce twisters. It was an El Niño year, when the cyclical warming of Pacific Ocean waters had climatologists across the globe measuring its effects on rainfall, temperature, and trade winds. No sooner had meteorologists in the United States begun to wonder about El Niño's influences on the spring tornado season when the first deadly outbreak occurred in central Florida shortly before midnight on February 22.

It was the worst time of day for a storm to hit. Seven tornadoes spun through the state as most people slept, oblivious to the vicious skies above them. At the Ponderosa Recreational Vehicle Park near Kissimmee, white lightning lit up the night as snowbirds, the retirees who escape winters in colder climates by driving their trailers to Florida, settled in for the night. A rodeo was in town and had kept many of the travelers lingering in the area. In the sky, the lightning turned blue and then the sound of a bomb ripped though the trailer park. One resident looked out the window of his RV and saw pieces of a nearby convenience store fly by. His own life was over, he told himself. But somehow he and his wife survived. Twenty-four people in the park and in nearby Morningside Acres Mobile Home Park did not have the same luck. It took three days to dig through the debris and recover all of the bodies. The final tally for the seven-storm spree was forty-two lives in four counties. More than 250 people suffered injuries. The National Weather Service would call the spree the deadliest outbreak in the state's history. The second worst tornado outbreak hit the state on March 31, 1962, claiming the lives of seventeen people, less than half of the number of people killed in 1998's midnight attack.

Less than a month after the deadly February tornado, another tornado paraded through Georgia for thirteen miles and killed eighteen people in two counties northeast of Atlanta. In early morning hours, high winds tossed a tractor-trailer into a school, killing the driver. Had the tornado hit an hour later than it did, it could have taken the lives of children arriving at school for the start of a new day. The same storm system spun off a tornado that killed two people in North Carolina and damaged close to six hundred homes.

A few days later, on March 29, nearly two-dozen tornadoes swept through the Upper Midwest and left two people dead, including a six-year-old boy who was sucked from the van he was riding in and tossed into a muddy field. One hundred people in the town of Comfrey, Minnesota were left homeless.

One week after the April 8 disaster in Jefferson County, tornadoes tormented the Mississippi and Tennessee valleys every day for seven days. A tornado on April 16 killed two people in a mobile home near Ro Ellen, Tennessee, and then killed two more people in nearby Manila. Storms later that day moved through Tennessee, Mississippi, and Arkansas, taking the lives of ten other residents. One funnel cloud that was part of that system took a stunning turn through Nashville shortly before the evening rush hour. More than one hundred people suffered injuries, and in its six-mile path, the storm damaged three hundred buildings, including the State Capitol.

On May 30, only a dozen homes still stood in Spencer, South Dakota after a half-mile-wide funnel cloud barreled though the town. The tornado stayed on the ground for twenty-one miles, but had its path taken it a quarter-mile north or south, much of the three-hundred-population prairie town would still exist. Six people died and 150 others were injured. A grain elevator, the post office, the fire station, the library, the bank, and the town's four churches were reduced to shredded boards. The winds shoved a tractor-trailer into a tree and crushed the town's water tower to the ground, where it lay with dents kicked in it. One couple's wedding photos were found hundreds of miles away.

Since the April 8 tornado, Terry Hyche had thrown himself into his work. While Chief Tim Love and another firefighter hammered out the details of the new Station Three's construction, Terry researched and ordered equipment. In just a few weeks' time, he had ordered turnout gear, two new pumper trucks, and other much-needed equipment. He compared prices for phone service, cable TV, and computers. He found out that inmates in Alabama's prison system made furniture, and decided that since the legislature had given the district money to rebuild, it would be a nice gesture to reinvest that money in a state project. When the other firefighters agreed, he ordered the prison-made tables and chairs. Much of the new equipment had to be stored in Terry's patched-up garage until Station Three was built. But every time UPS dropped off another package, he felt the fire district was that much closer to being a fully functioning department once again. It felt like Christmas when he saw that brown truck, he told the other rescuers.

Work was more than a comfort to him. When he flipped through the catalogs of rescue gear, he didn't have to think about what more he could have done for his family or for the injured on the night of the storm. The harder Terry worked, the more praise he got for his efforts, and Chief Love made him an assistant chief for his efforts. That pleased Terry even more, and he kept up the heavy workload, spending as much of his spare time as he could on the fire district's rebuilding efforts.

In the months after the storm, he got a new partner, Curtis Poe. They were an odd pair: Terry, the easygoing son of a Baptist minister, and Curtis, the rapid-fire, macho guy who served as a paratrooper in the Persian Gulf War. Terry never drank a drop of liquor in his life and Curtis was a reformed drug user. But they got along well and even started socializing outside the station with their families.

For Curtis Poe, little in his life seemed to change after the storm. Every third day, he ran calls at the engine company in Birmingham, and every third day he saw death. He had come to accept that. That was the cold nature of his job. Usually it was somebody whose heart gave out or who went face first into his steering wheel of his car. Somebody circling the drain, he would joke, somebody who had "The Q" on his face, as in "The Question"—"Why they hell did I just die?" Once he ran on a car wreck that tore up a guy so badly, Curtis nearly stepped on the man's kidney. At least, that's how he joked about it back at the station. He didn't mean any harm, but he had seen too many cut-up bodies to get too worked up about this guy's injuries.

When he was a rookie, Curtis used to run from the ambulance to his patients, like the firefighters on "Rescue 911." He would get to the scene, catapult himself out of the ambulance like a bullet out of a gun, and then sprint across the front yard to his patient. He got there quick all right. But he was so out of breath that he had to pause before he could do any medical work. These days, he walked. Quickly, but he walked nonetheless.

Rescue work was nothing like TV. Not every patient could be saved, even with CPR. And the ones that did live never came back and took Curtis to the zoo, or bought him a hot dog. Sure, it was important work and on the best of days it was work that could make a person proud. Before the tornado, Curtis pulled a ten-month-old baby from a burning house in Birmingham and saved the child's life. Few other accomplishments in his life could compare to that triumph. But those moments were rare.

Curtis liked being a rescuer because he liked knowing what to do in bad situations. He liked being in control, and usually he made things work out the way he wanted. Sometimes, like in the case of Nathan Seals, he didn't. For two hours, he kept Nathan alive as they tried to get the boy out of that mess. He bagged him with a mask, put air in his lungs, begged him to stay alive, and for what? The kid died a few days later. Curtis had a lot of training, a lot of know-how. He was strong and he gave all of himself that night. But in the end it didn't matter. There was nothing he could do about it, though. He just had to put it out of his mind and keep moving. There was no use in dwelling on something that he couldn't change. He wondered if it was possible for a soul to get so bruised that a callous could grow around it.

"Hard-hearted," his wife spit at him one day. He was hard-hearted about death. Why, he never even paid a deceased person his respects at a funeral, not so much as took a step toward the casket.

Curtis couldn't deny that. But he told his Cassandra, "Look you don't understand. Every third day, I have to look at that. Every third day, somebody's dying around me. After awhile you just get sick and tired of it. You know in the end that's the end result for everybody, but after you've seen it so much, you get tired of looking at it."

"Why don't you share this stuff with me?" she yelled at him.

But he never could bring himself to tell her about his work, especially what he saw on the night of the tornado. He couldn't tell how hard it was to stay calm when everybody around him screamed for help, how there was so little the fire-fighters could do, how the adrenaline rushed through his body as the other rescuers leaned on his expertise and his combat experience, or how scared and helpless he felt as he held Nathan's broken body in the cab of the pickup truck. Curtis just couldn't tell Cassandra how pissed off he was in the hospital when the nurse told him the boy he had struggled to save, a boy he had never really known anyway, had died. He had been so mad he would have liked to punch somebody. It wouldn't have made him feel better, of course. He knew that. It wouldn't have done a damn bit of good and then he would have to tell Cassanrda how useless he felt, how powerless. He didn't even want to think about any of this. Death, loss, helplessness. So he just kept his mouth shut. Let my heart get hard, he thought. The less said, the better.

Eddie Clark, a volunteer firefighter in Cranston Heights, Delaware, had watched with horror on that April day as pictures of the chaos in Concord filled his TV screen. Eddie had never seen anything like it—the number of houses destroyed, the churches split apart, the fire stations obliterated. For emergency workers—the very people who help in a time of crisis—to lose nearly everything themselves seemed like a cruel fate. But it had gotten Clark thinking.

The Cranston Heights Volunteer Fire Department had been trying to sell a 1978 Mack CF pumper, with no luck. The truck was in good shape and it sure looked like the boys in Alabama needed it. Perhaps the fire department could donate it to them. Clark told Chief Jim Scholl about his idea and the chief liked it. He called Chief Tim Love in Alabama and asked him if he wanted a free truck.

At first, Chief Love didn't know what to say. Another fire company wanted to give them a truck? That sure was something. Of course, he accepted the offer.

That spring, a C-130 troop carrier arrived in Birmingham with Scholl, Clark, and the Mack pumper. Neighboring fire departments in Delaware's New Castle County added to the gift by contributing boots, helmets, and other needed equipment. Some of the items came with a simple, unsigned note that said, "Hope this will help." The Concord firefighters had no names but the departments' own to thank.

Birmingham TV stations sent reporters to cover the truck's arrival. For months after the tornado, local news broadcasts regularly featured updates on the beleaguered fire district and its two lost stations. The story made the national media as well. At first, the firefighters cautiously courted the attention. Like everyone affected by the disaster, they had stories to tell and reporters wanted to listen. Then, in one report, Chief Love was described as sitting pitifully on a curb across from Station Three with his head in his hands, woefully wondering out loud how the department would ever rebuild. It was a characterization that he strongly objected to. He would readily admit there were tense moments after he discovered the district was underinsured. But he never felt like he indulged in self-pity. He didn't like to be too critical though. Ever the optimist, he thought some good came from all the media attention. Without the nationwide disaster coverage, Chief Love believed the fire district would not have received the help that it did.

Oddly enough, as the pumper arrived in Birmingham, Chief Love was in Washington, D.C., meeting with members of the Congressional Fire Institute and to symbolically take ownership of the district's new truck from the Delaware chiefs who were gathered at the meeting. Chief Love, whose tab for the trip was picked up by several businesses, ordered a special dress uniform for the occasion. He had never needed one before. He spoke to two different groups of firefighters about the rescue work on the night of the storm. After one of his talks, a firefighter dropped some money in his hat and then passed it to the other men and women in the room. When the cap returned, it held $5,000.

There were other gifts, too. A fire company in North Carolina sent twenty-three air packs that were in good condition. One new pack alone would have cost the Concord district $4,000. The Jefferson County Firefighters Association donated $1,000, and the Alabama State Firemen's Association gave the district $1,300. A wealthy rescue buff from Colorado sent a $25,000 thermal imaging device that could be used to find bodies or survivors in a smoke-filled building. Karns, a fire equipment manufacturer, gave the district's rescuers thirty new helmets.

Smaller, but equally meaningful, donations poured in, too. One day an elderly woman who lived in Bessemer called Station One and told one of the firefighters she had heard about their tornado damage and that she would like to give the firefighters a little money. But she had no way to get to Concord. A firefighter who worked in Bessemer stopped by her house and picked up a check for $100. The woman, who looked like she lived on a fixed income, didn't know anybody who lived in the fire district. Nor did she know any firefighters. She just wanted to help the rescuers.

This generosity amazed Chief Love. He knew firefighters stuck together. But for somebody to give them a truck, and then for people they didn't even know, people who sure could use the money themselves, to give something to the district, well, that was just something. It was one of the few times the talkative chief didn't know what to say. He took the gifts and offered what he could, his humble thanks.

Meanwhile, he started accepting invitations to speak from organizations all over the country. He spoke to a group of rescuers in Colorado, and then, in late September, went to Delaware with Richie Miller and firefighter Mike Chaney as guests of the state volunteer firefighters association. They visited Cranston Heights, in the suburbs of Wilmington, to visit the fire department that gave Concord the old pumper five months earlier. There, they were greeted like long-lost kin. Everyone wanted to shake hands with the boys from Alabama, the ones who made it through that storm. Eddie Clark, the firefighter who first thought of giving Concord the department's old truck, shyly deferred any attention. But Mike Chaney, who carried a large camera and flash, snapped pictures of Clark, as well as of the brick fire station. It was inconceivable—a brick fire station, and one for volunteers, at that. "This here is a Taj Mahal," Mike told Clark. "Y'all got yourselves a Taj Mahal." After the tour, a Cranston Heights volunteer whisked the Concord firefighters around Wilmington in a red fire department Suburban like heroes in a chariot. From the back seat, Chief Love and Richie shouted friendly "Hey y'alls" to women on the street.

That night, Chief Love spoke at a dinner for fire chiefs from around the state. It was only the second time he wore his dress uniform, but his public speaking skills were polished. He told the crowd how firefighter Scott Swindle rode out the storm in a rescue truck. Then he showed a slide of a large section of a house blown one mile from its foundation. The audience gasped. Afterward, a crowd gathered around Chief Love and souvenirs were pressed into the Concord firefighters' hands. By the end of the evening, Chief Love was holding two hats, two T-shirts, a mug, and an arm patch. More offers of equipment and trucks were made. Somewhat emotional, Chief Love announced, "After today, we consider that we have a thousand friends in Delaware."

Despite the gifts and nationwide attention, all was not well at home. For one, the fire district still faced insurmountable debts. Money had been more than tight, and even before the tornado the fire district expected to be $20,000 in the hole for 1998. Earlier in the year, a citizens committee had studied ways for the district to cut costs and increase revenue. By some accounts, the committee recommended raising annual dues by twenty dollars a household. Others believed the number was closer to twelve dollars. In the days after the disaster, Concord Fire District's Board of Directors voted to increase the annual dues from $120 to $160 per household.

But when the fire district received a free pumper, truckloads of new equipment, and a promise for $740,000 from the state, people objected to the $40 per household raise. Yes, the firefighters needed to build two new stations, but they weren't the only ones who were hurting. Just how much more did these guys want, people asked. A petition circulated around Concord, Rock Creek, and Oak Grove. More than 300 people signed the paper, which asked the county circuit court to halt the dues increase until September 1 when a general election could decide the issue.

This was a backlash the firefighters never expected. As a result, they started touting their success stories. For weeks, their eyes had darkened and their voices had choked when they talked about the people they couldn't save on the night of the storm. Their pain was so raw it felt like an extra piece of equipment they strapped to their backs and carried with them every day. But now they talked about the victories, the people they had saved, and they talked about how so many of them had left their own homes and their own families to help the community. Kathy Hyche proudly remembered how a woman stopped her in Wal-Mart in the days after the tornado and told her that when she had heard Terry's voice on her fire radio that night she took cover in the bathroom. Had the woman stayed in living room, listening to her radio, she would have likely died. Terry Hyche had saved her life.

They did their jobs, the firefighters argued, and they didn't waste money. They pointed to their part-time chief and his $6.25-an-hour salary. His hourly earnings were less than what a nearby Taco Bell paid some of its workers. If Chief Tim Love worked full time for the district, he would likely pull in a salary of $30,000 to $40,000 a year. The firefighters agreed they would rather spend money on equipment than pay. They felt they took the district's best interests to heart.

Many of them were former mechanics that cut costs by spending their free Saturdays repairing the district's trucks instead of sending them out to be fixed. Technically, they violated federal labor law every time they did this. Firefighters were not supposed to volunteer for the same departments that paid them. But this was the kind of place where people sealed deals with a handshake. Until the flap over the dues, some of the rescuers who knew better figured there was no harm in letting folks pitch in when that was the way it had been done for so long. It was all for the good of the district anyway.

But as the controversy grew, rumors spread that firefighters did so much work themselves because it was a way for them to pad their expenses and get extra money for the department. They jacked up equipment prices when it actually would have been cheaper to take their fire engines to a garage. One angry resident wrote into a local paper, agreeing that the district saved money by employing a part-time chief. But she charged that it paid benefits and pensions to firefighters who worked elsewhere and got those perks from their full-time jobs. By July, the district had received $19,000 in cash donations from local residents and businesses. Much of the money went into the firefighter's fund, which was used specifically to purchase new equipment. That further angered some of the petition-signers. If the district was going to fall $20,000 short in meeting its annual expenses, it made sense for the board to set aside some of the donations to patch up this budget hole.

A circuit court judge considered the residents' petition and told the fire district's board to renegotiate with the committee. Both sides met. They agreed to raise dues $20, and the petition was dropped. But bitterness lingered. It was hard for some residents to believe that the firefighters deserved the special treatment, the media attention, and the donations from around the country when so many other people had been affected by the same storm. Sure, these rescuers saved lives that night. But that was their job. That was what residents paid them $120 per household each year to do.

At the same time, the firefighters felt they were unfairly targeted, that their board, the only elected body in the district, had become the lightning rod for the community's discontent. It was true that as everyone bandaged their wounds and worked through the stress of recovery, people had grown angry. Some raged at the weather, at God, at themselves, and at their neighbors. Others chose the fire-fighters. What better target for this fury than the people who were supposed to save lives, but who had found themselves at the mercy of this storm, too?

The less her husband talked about the tornado, the less Cassandra Poe knew how to talk to him. The less she talked to him, the less he said to her. Round and round this went until their marriage felt like a smoldering building with no fire escape.

Even without a disaster, it was hard to be married to a firefighter. No one told this to spouses before they tossed the rice and wished the couple well. Instead, rescue workers were played up as a good catch. They were macho. They saved lives. Women bought calendars of muscular firemen posing in their turnout gear and helmets. What nobody ever told Cassandra was that Curtis might have enough courage to run into a burning building, but that he also wouldn't be home most of the time. He worked one twenty-four-hour shift in Birmingham, was home for a day, and then worked another twenty-four-hour shift for Concord. His workdays were long ones for Cassandra. She had to be mom and dad, plus maid, cook, and handyman. Even before the tornado, Curtis's schedule caused problems.

"Where's Daddy?" Taylor always asked. "Why does he have to work?"

When he was home, Curtis tried to help around the house. But it was hard for him to find the time to get things done. Cassandra resented him. He felt like she was a nag. Arguments about taking out the trash exploded often and lasted longer than they should have. Some days they didn't talk much to each other at all.

After the tornado, Curtis grew angrier. Cassandra could see that. But she felt that he had every right to be. He had been though so much, from the death of his sister to the storm that changed the community. Hard times stuck to him like the air he breathed. It was almost as if the good Lord knew Curtis could handle a bad situation, so he kept giving him more. Curtis's job in Birmingham frustrated Curtis, too. Some days when he came home from the station, he would tell her about a patient with a stomachache or a bad knee who had called the ambulance because he wanted to make sure his insurance covered his ailment, or because he was too lazy to drive himself to the hospital. Curtis had the same complaint that many urban paramedics do—people were abusing the system. After the tornado, it was hard for him to muster any sympathy for these patients, even if they didn't know any better. That night in Rock Creek, there were people who desperately needed his help, who cried out to him and held onto him as he carried them to an ambulance. But his patients in Birmingham caused their own problems. Hell, he figured about ninety percent of the wounds he healed and the pains he took away were self-inflicted. If a man smoked all of his life, then it was his fault he had a heart attack. If a kid lived his life wrong, then it was no surprise that he got shot two or three times.

Cassandra understood some of what her husband went through, but she didn't know what to say to make him feel better about it. He didn't know how to tell her what he needed. They separated, got back together again, and separated again. In the end, both of them blamed his job.

Weeks after the deadly 1998 season blew to a close, disaster experts, meteorologists, and wind engineers gathered in Washington, D.C. to talk about storm safety. Overall, improved forecasting and warning systems had decreased the number of tornado-related deaths in the second half of the century. But nearly everyone at the two-day meetings agreed that more work needed to be done.

Scientists talked about Doppler radar improvements and about the need for more storm spotters, volunteers such as Eddie Maxwell, who could provide meteorologists with a real-life weather picture. Other experts promoted weather warning radios, and engineers from Texas Tech University's Wind Engineering Research Center unveiled a plan to educate the public about in-residence tornado shelters, storm-safe hideaways that can be constructed on the first floor of homes without basements.

Other work that year focused on the structure of tornadoes. Researchers from the University of Oklahoma chased storms with a mobile Doppler radar, known as Doppler on Wheels, to get a better look at the makeup of funnel clouds and their wind speeds. Although University of Oklahoma researchers had used different mobile and portable radar since the late 1980s, scientists first used the Doppler on Wheels in 1995, when they were able to record data on a spring tornado. A year later, they took the Doppler on Wheels to North Carolina where it measured the wind speeds of Hurricane Fran as it slammed into the coast. In the data they collected, they discovered boundary-layer rolls, or helical shapes that spiraled horizontally in the hurricane in alternating streaks of higher and lower wind speeds. Winds in one roll might blow at one hundred miles per hour, while another roll might have winds speeds of sixty miles per hour. Almost two months after the April 8 tornado, researchers used the portable Doppler to record 245 mile-per-hour wind speeds near Spencer, South Dakota, when a tornado destroyed the entire town. This marked one of the few times the wind speed of a tornado was measured and later crosschecked with the ensuing damage that occurred in the area. Scientists first accomplished that was in Los Alamos, New Mexico in 1991. However, in almost every case after the introduction of the Fujita scale, tornado damage had been the only means to calculate the storm's strength.

In Alabama, Jefferson County Commissioner Mary Buckelew signed an agreement with the Federal Emergency Management Agency (FEMA) to make the once tornado-ravaged community stronger against the brutal force of disaster. FEMA in turn provided $150,000 in seed money for proposals that would reduce the loss of life and property when the next disaster hit Jefferson County. The seed money paid for an improved early warning system and an emergency information website. It also was used to hire a coordinator who encouraged business and citizen involvement in the effort. Fifteen people from government, emergency management, the National Weather Service, and the community at large formed a board of directors and began to analyze the county's risk for tornadoes, flooding, terrorism, and other disasters. At the same time, people began talking about the next generation—the kids who had lived through this storm and who would grow up to become scientists, rescue workers, and emergency managers. Terry Hyche wondered if his son David might become a meteorologist one day. That could be the storm's legacy, he felt, the story worth talking about after everyone finally put aside their pain and suffering.

Christie Seals covered her face with her hands and prayed. "God, my life is like something out of the newspaper." Sometimes it was just too much to think about how her family's home and everything in it had been destroyed, how she had suffered from a punctured lung and a severely broken leg, how her husband Matthew was paralyzed, and how their son Nathan was dead. On most days, she only let herself think about one sorrow at a time, because that was all she could handle. She would think about losing Nathan and only that. Other times, she would mourn for the family's house or for Matthew's health. But she stopped herself before she thought about anything else. Otherwise she would become overwhelmed. She couldn't do that. She had to keep going. For John Michael's and Margaret's sake, at least. They had lost Nathan and she didn't want her two little ones to lose their childhoods, too.

In the weeks after the storm, Christie and Matthew talked about returning to Rock Creek and building a bigger house, one with a storm shelter. It was a conversation that lasted only a few minutes before the couple decided they needed to start over. Rock Creek was not the same; their neighborhood was ruined and many of their neighbors were gone, including Miss Williams, who had always found some excuse to come out and talk to them at the bus stop. Christie and Matthew had not planned on living in Rock Creek for a long time anyway. They had bought their house with the hopes of fixing it up and selling it five years later. Still, Matthew worried that by not going back to Rock Creek the family would be running away from what happened to them. Christie told him, no, they were moving on.

She found an apartment for the family to live in, and Matthew finally came home from a rehabilitation center in July. But by then, it was clear to Christie that the couple's marriage was over. Depressed and overwhelmed she could no longer cope with the losses and all of her grief; on some days she felt so much grief it was almost like another person was in the house. They could set a place at the table for it, make up a spare bed. This pain wasn't going away.

Matthew, however, was. Less than a month after he returned home from the hospital, Christie asked him to move out. He was shocked. "It's like you're in a battle and you're in a foxhole and all of the sudden the guy next to you turns his gun on you," he told friends. Right now, he felt that he and Christie needed each other more than ever. They needed to pull together for the sake of their family. She didn't think so. For him, Christie's rejection proved harder to deal with than being in a wheelchair. He didn't like being in wheelchair but he understood why he was and he prayed nightly about his injuries. "God, if this is the way it's going to be, I don't understand it. But let something good come out of it." He prayed for Christie, too.

Christie spent the next several months looking for a house for her and the children, a one-level house with doors large enough for Matthew to wheel himself through. He was gone out of her life, she was pretty sure of that, but she didn't want him out of John Michael and Margaret's life. The house also had to have a basement where Christie could hide with the children the next time a strong wind blew. She found a thirty-year-old house in Hoover and she and the two kids moved into it in December.

The house was a lot nicer than their home in Rock Creek. Shady oak trees, like the ones at their old place, flanked three sides, and the back yard had plenty of running room for two children. But this home was not a fixer-upper. There was little inside its brick walls that needed repairing. There was a good-sized living room and a family room that stretched across the back of the house. Plenty of kitchen space, too. It was perfect.

For a while, Christie was excited. Then she lost the thrill of a new house. She stood in the kitchen, making dinner for the kids and longing for her old clothes, the sheets she used to slept on, the toys John Michael and Margaret used to play with. All of it was lost in the storm, except for one chair, two blankets, and a scrapbook's worth of photographs. The newness of everything made her tense. She couldn't turn off her alarm clock, traipse across her bedroom floor, and step into the bathroom every morning without seeing a room full of things she didn't own months before. It made it impossible for her to forget about the tornado.

Her work at Children's Hospital would comfort her. That's what she told herself. She never had time to think when she tended the little ones who so desperately needed her help. Before the storm, she could lose herself for hours watching somebody else's babies. She used to believe that the care she gave a dying child was her way of helping the parents. She would do right for the mother and father by caring for their son or daughter in the way she would want one of her own to be looked after. She grieved for the parents who lost a child, but she was a professional. She never stepped over the line. Her job always came before her feelings.

In the fall, she went back to work at the intensive care unit, the same unit where she had held her son's hand and kissed him goodbye. Although Matthew had been in favor of moving back to Rock Creek, he opposed Christie's return to the intensive care unit. He worried that it would be too much for her too soon, and that perhaps she was in denial about how painful it would be to be back on the same unit where their son died. In her first weeks back, it was obvious to Christie that her job wasn't providing the solace for which she had longed. So many of the patients reminded her of Nathan, other little boys, kids with head injuries, children so close to letting go of their last breath. Every time she treated a patient like this she thought of her son. It became harder for her to shoulder a parent's grief without feeling her own. She began to empathize, not like a nurse, but like a mother.

Friends told her to quit her job, that she had nothing to prove. But she disagreed. "I have to prove to myself that I can do it still," she told them. Her coworkers didn't mention the tornado to her for fear of reminding her of her loss. But that didn't matter. She never stopped thinking about it. The first time she went to the grocery store after the storm, she broke down crying when she remembered how Nathan always held a bag for her as she ground her favorite coffee. Once in a McDonald's she saw a child who looked so much like him that she watched the boy for five minutes, just to make sure it was not her son.

"There he is. He's just disappeared for awhile," she told herself.

Later, she asked Children's Hospital for the photo they took of Nathan in the trauma room on the night of the storm, the one the emergency room workers used to identify him. It ended up being the last picture taken of Nathan, and

Christie wanted to have it. To hold it in her hand and look at it made his death seem more real. She would sit in her new house in Hoover, on the plush green sofa a furniture store had donated, and sift through pictures that neighbors and friends salvaged from the rubble on Hancock Drive. She looked at pictures of Nathan in a tree or Nathan in costume, a photo of her holding his chubby diapered body on her lap. Her hair cut short and wavy, in the fashion of the early '90s, her face was as innocent as his. Then she would look at that last photo from Children's Hospital. "If looking at photos brought someone back," she thought, "Nathan would be here now."

Months after the tornado, storm spotter Eddie Maxwell ran on a call for a brush fire and realized with a shock that nearly every firefighter working the blaze was either fighting with or separated from his wife. Only he and Patricia were still together. Marital problems had become epidemic in the fire district. Was it because of the tornado? He wondered.

Seven months after the tornado and five months after they moved into their new mobile home, Melanie Miller took her daughter Christina and left Richie. He didn't think she was ever coming back. This was the second time the couple had separated during their short marriage, and Richie felt like another tornado had knocked the wind out of him. His preacher visited him at Station One and together they prayed in the tiny office behind the fire trucks. Richie knew where he had been at fault. After the tornado, he never sat down with Melanie and talked about the storm and everything they lost. He never held her in his arms and told her it would be OK. He should have done that. But he didn't even stay to comfort them and Christina on the night of the storm. As Melanie cried over the house, he turned on his fire radio and then left. "I deserted them," he told his minister.

Richie called Melanie and begged her to come back. He begged her to let him see Christina. He hoped they would get back together by Christmas, but as the days passed, he knew he would spend the holiday alone.

It was clear that others struggled with their families and their feelings. One guilt-ridden firefighter cried every time he talked about Nathan Seals and contemplated quitting his post with the department until Chief Tim Love intervened and got him to talk to a counselor. Another firefighter found religion and had a tornado tattooed on his arm. Despite his insistence that he was coping well, friends worried that he wasn't.

The survivors still wrestled with the question of why, why they lived when others died, why they were even hit by a tornado at all. One man wondered why he hadn't stepped into his car and sped out of Rock Creek when the sky clouded over to an eerie green. Why did he stay when he had the chance to leave? The storm was too big, his father told him. That was why none of them left. There was no way to escape it. There was nothing anybody could have done to prevent the storm. They couldn't stab it, shoot it, threaten it, or do anything else that would stop it. None of them had any control over what was about to happen.

Christmas came and went without a tree in either the cramped Station One in Concord or the makeshift station in Oak Grove. December 25 seemed to be buried at the back of everyone's minds. The firefighters still held their annual parade, where a rescuer rode around each of the district's three communities and tossed candy to the kids. But getting back to normal life—rebuilding the two demolished stations—still occupied much of the rescuers' thoughts.

In Oak Grove, firefighters continued to run calls out of a rented trailer. Salvaged tables from the Oak Grove School, one of them bearing the carved message, "Tisia loves Damon," and other hand-me-downs lent a musty odor to the place. Residents had donated a coffee maker, a microwave, and dishes, and one firefighter's mother, who lost her antique store in the storm, had given the firefighters her refrigerator. Still, there was nothing friendly or welcoming about this station. The rescuers ate their meals at a table salvaged from the demolished Oak Grove school and washed their dishes in the tiny bathroom sink, an arrangement many of them considered unsanitary. Green garbage bags made window shades. On the walls, scrawled signs from Chief Tim Love warned the firefighters not to leave their spit cups around the trailer and urged the rescuers to familiarize themselves with newly arrived equipment. Then, just before Christmas a cold snap froze the trailer's pipes, and the toilet stopped working. A new fire station topped everyone's wish list.

But now, it was obvious the new Station Three would not be completed by January 1 as predicted. Everyone hoped to be in the building by February, but even that looked doubtful. With many of the storm's survivors rebuilding their homes or businesses, permit requests clogged the county, and the paperwork backlog was unprecedented. Even in the best of circumstances, putting up a new fire station could take a while. Materials and supplies had to be ordered in between emergency calls, and important decisions were made only in the down time. But in this case, nothing could happen fast enough.

Hoping to keep up morale, Chief Love spread tile samples and paint chips across a table at Station One and asked the other men for their opinions. With a wrestling match on the TV and the fast food wrappers from the day's lunch at their elbows, a few of the firefighters studied the colors like women at a makeup counter. The chief knew that most of the men didn't care if beige or blue tile covered the floors. But he wanted them to stay excited about the new station, to be hopeful about the good times that surely lay ahead.

Gray clouds, the color of gun metal, gathered in the sky above Rock Creek, and the wind's whistle turned to a whine. Slow and soft at first, the nagging grew to a near taunt as the wind wrapped itself around the few houses left in its path. The rains that followed drenched the ground in easy, even showers. But Patricia Maxwell felt nervous. Every time it rained or when the wind whined in that menacing way, she found herself uneasily watching from the window. Since the tornado, she couldn't bare to look at the reminders that lingered everywhere, on the scarred hillside they could see from their yard, in the splintered trees that used to shield them from the traffic sounds on Warrior River Road. Everywhere around her she saw sadness.

Her doctor diagnosed her with depression and she began to take pills to help her feel like her old self. Friends who meant well tried to cheer her up by saying that she had been blessed. After all, she and Eddie had survived the storm, and their house sustained little damage. But Patricia didn't like to hear that kind of talk. Why had they been blessed when their neighbors, the Browns and the Sauters, had lost their lives? Storms weren't God's way of blessing or punishing. They were something that couldn't be explained.

She was grateful for Eddie's love and support. He understood her sad spells and didn't treat her like she was losing her mind. He loved her as he always had, unconditionally. Then, weeks before the one-year anniversary of the storm, Eddie lost his job when Jim Walter Resources Inc. closed a mine near Oak Grove. After twenty years as a coal miner and only one year away from collecting his pension, Eddie was out of work. And he was fifty, not an easy age for finding a job. He, too, grew depressed.

In the days after the tornado, Eddie and Patricia had found a Teddy bear face down in the mud as they combed through debris in their backyard. Patricia washed it, brushed its fur, and fluffed it back up. They called it their storm bear. They didn't know how to find the kid who owned the bear. But they thought about that little boy or girl every time they looked at the stuffed animal and they prayed the child was all right.

It was a small gesture to save the toy, but it felt bigger and right somehow to hold onto something the tornado had spared. They longed for their lives as they were before the storm. Eddie felt as if they had been robbed of what they had.

They weren't going to get it back, he knew. They kept what they could, a tiny bear.

Ironically, as the firefighters bandaged together the pieces of their shattered personal lives, they were once again noticed professionally. At the end of 1998, the Birmingham Regional Emergency Medical Services named Chief Tim Love the EMT of the year for Jefferson County, largely because of the Concord Fire District's efforts in the hours after the tornado. At an awards ceremony, Tarrant Fire Chief Billy Hewitt told the audience how hard Chief Love and the other firefighters had worked and how well they had done their jobs that night. Hewitt had heard Chief Love speak in Washington, D.C. less than a month after the tornado when he told more than one thousand people at the Congressional Fire Institute dinner how he and the other rescuers struggled and how much more they wished they could have done to help their community. Wearing his dress uniform for the first time, Chief Love looked to Hewitt like "he'd rather take a whipping" than talk to the crowd of senators, lobbyists, and even James Lee Witt, director of the Federal Emergency Management Agency. But the chief forgot his nerves as he started talking about the four firefighters who lost their homes, the fourteen people who lost their lives, and the demolished school, where hundreds of students could have been killed had the tornado hit hours earlier. He easily won the audience's heart. Hewitt, who retired from the Birmingham Fire Department as assistant chief in 1995, always thought Chief Love showed a lot of promise as a firefighter. But after the tornado, he told the audience at the EMT award ceremony, he considered the young chief to be one of his heroes.

A year after the tornado, the pounding of hammers stopped. Fewer cars were braking on Warrior River road so the occupants could gawk and sigh. The sounds of kids gleefully shrieking, dogs barking, and cars motoring to and from neighborhoods resumed. There were signs of new life in the new year. Fresh, cheerful houses dotted the once-desolate landscape. Assistant Chief Robbie Miller and his family moved into their new home, across from where Station Two would be rebuilt, and the two-story house looked like a shiny doll's house as it towered over the flattened remains of the tornado's destructive binge along Warrior River Road. In general, this crop of new homes was bigger and nicer than what the tornado took. The homes were brick instead of wood frame, and they showed off a new optimism. People not only were coming back to Concord, they were coming back to stay. That made the large, sunny houses that brightened the sad, empty streets an even more welcome sight. Across from the old Station Three, saws swished through boards and drills buzzed as a young couple built a replica of the Victorian they had spent years repairing and then lost to the storm.

For Curtis and Cassandra Poe, there was a new beginning as well. After another one of their separations, they had recently reconciled. Curtis stopped seeing a girl he dated while he and Cassandra were apart and moved back home. He helped around the house as much as he could and spent more time with the girls. Five-year-old Taylor wanted to be a firefighter, just like her daddy. Curtis wasn't so keen on seeing rescue work become a family business. He would never want her to witness all the bad things he had seen on the job. But he liked that his daughter wasn't a prissy, ribbon-in-the-hair type. He would be proud if Taylor fought fires.

Happy times had found the Poe house. Caught up in the giddiness of the family's fresh start, Curtis even gave up his nearly lifelong tobacco habit. Cassandra talked about trying for another baby, hopefully a boy this time.

Soon, there was a reason for everyone to celebrate. Ten months after the tornado, Station Three was finally finished. The firefighters locked up the old trailer in Oak Grove and began running calls out of the butler-style building that was so new the smell of fresh paint filled its rooms. To Concord's rescuers, this station was just as much a Taj Mahal as the fancy brick station they saw in Delaware. Outside, flashy red siding rose up from the cinder block foundation. Inside, the three truck bays were bigger than the old station itself. Plus, there was a gigantic day room, a classroom on the building's second floor, and so much office space that for the first time Tim Love had his own office. Pleased the building was finally in service, he spent the first few weeks giving tours to anybody who showed up, from the citizens who would be protected by the people and equipment in this new building to the politicians who wanted to see how the state's money was being spent.

Then, on an unseasonably hot and sun-scarring day one year and two days after the April 1998 tornado, the Concord Fire District dedicated the new Station Three. One hundred people—a smaller crowd than hoped for—gathered outside the bright red building and listened to a stage full of politicians talk about shattered buildings and unbroken spirits. Near the platform, the ranks of Concord's paid rescuers and volunteers stood at attention behind the two assistant chiefs, Robbie Miller and Terry Hyche, who wore spangled dress uniforms for the occasion. On the platform sat several firefighters from the Delaware stations that had donated equipment to the Alabama rescuers they had seen on TV.

Firefighters from both states wiped tears from their eyes as a minister read "A Firemen's Prayer." Its words rhymed like a greeting card, but still held a lot of meaning for the rescue workers. "…Enable me to be alert and Hear the weakest shout, And quickly and efficiently, To put the fire out, I want to fill my calling and, To give the best in me, To guard my every neighbor, And protect their property." There were prayers for the people who died and prayers of thanks for the new station. Chief Tim Love unveiled a monument to the fourteen district residents who lost their lives in the storm. Then, in a proud moment, he cut the ribbon that stretched across the front of the building, and three firefighters drove trucks out of the brand-new bays in a well-timed flourish of flashing lights.

The ceremony felt as all-American as a barn raising or a Fourth of July parade. Cassandra Poe and other wives sold T-shirts with a green funnel cloud on the back and the words, "F-5+, Off the Scale." The men served their guests barbecue they had spent two days cooking. Camera flashes snapped as bright as the sun and people clapped each other on the back. Curious residents toured the spacious station and a few of the firefighters strutted around like baseball players after a hard-won victory. At last, they had their station. This was what they had wanted for so long. This was what they needed to put the tornado behind them. They had told themselves when this day arrived that their lives would feel like they did before the storm.

But for all the anticipation, the day was hardly one of jubilation. Lips quivered beneath a few macho mustaches. People shielded their eyes from the glaring sky and from each other. Relatives sobbed next to the memorial. What was worse was that so many of the rescuers walked around with feelings that were as raw as they had been the day before.

Curtis Poe looked over the crowd for Christie Seals, but didn't see her. Both relief and regret filled him. He would have liked to offer his condolences at last, but he had to admit that he was afraid that meeting her would bring back bad memories. He might have even cried over them, and he wasn't real big on men crying. Besides, he didn't want anything dragging him down. He and Cassandra were still in a good patch, and for so many reasons, it was time to look to the future, to forge ahead. He was so tired of everyone belly-aching about the storm. Some of the men at the station just whined and whined about the tornado. Didn't they know they were grownups? They needed to move on. Once the hoo-rah of the ceremony was over with, he wanted to get back to the business of fire-fighting and forget about that damn F-5 forever.

At times when Nathan Seals or the boy's parents crept into his thoughts, Curtis reminded himself of how his parents felt when his sister Brandi was murdered.

She had been taken so quickly. She had left for school that morning as usual, then hours later she was dead. There had been no last goodbye. His parents never had a chance to make their peace with that, whatever peace could be made. At least Nathan's parents had the chance to hold his hand, to tell him they loved him, and to say goodbye. It had to make a difference, Curtis told himself. It had to. That was the best he could do.

Christie Seals did attend the dedication, although Curtis never saw her that day. It was another near miss between the two. She stood with the storm's other survivors, not knowing who Curtis was, or how hard he had tried to save her son's life. She shed some tears, looked at the monument that bore her son's name in a list of victims that looked sadly too long to her, and then went home. Soon, she would take a leave of absence from work at Children's Hospital so that her doctor could remove the pins that were put in her leg. After a two-month recovery, she planned on returning to the hospital's intensive care unit. Well-meaning friends and coworkers suggested that it was time for her to put in for a transfer. But she protested, "Every single thing in my life is brand new from my underwear to the dishes I eat on." She vowed to return to the intensive care unit.

There were few people at the ceremony who didn't know what had happened to Christie's family on the night of the storm. One young mother remembered hearing about Christie Seals lying out in the cold rain with her children scattered all around her, but unable to do anything to help them. A person could sit for hours and not come up with a worse torture for a mother, and the young woman thought about how easily it could have been her and her own child that night. It was a fear that haunted her so much that when a late afternoon storm threatened Rock Creek one spring day, she took the cloth belt from her bathrobe and tied her little girl's squirming body to her own. If anything happened, she wouldn't let go. She told herself she would hold her baby to her for hours if she had to.

There were other people hurting, too. Scott Swindle, who rode out the storm in a rescue truck, found himself in front of a TV every time bad weather threatened. Richie Miller remained separated from his wife. Eddie Maxwell was alone on this day, too. While the storm's rattling had done nothing to fracture the foundation of his marriage, Patricia still battled depression. She couldn't bring herself to attend the dedication ceremony, so that morning Eddie waved goodbye and drove off alone, feeling as lonely as he did on the night of the storm.

Terry Hyche, a newly minted assistant chief, found that he couldn't stop thinking about Baby Jessica, the little Texas girl who fell in a well in 1987 and whose rescue was broadcasted live on TV. Fame courted the unassuming men who saved her, and returning to their lives after the accident became an impossible feat. One of the rescuers, Robert O'Donnell, stopped trying to cope with the fickle nature of celebrity and took his own life in 1995. Just before his death, he had watched on TV the rescue effort after the Oklahoma City bombing. His story haunted Terry, who wondered what would happen once the Alabama firefighters no longer had the rebuilding of their stations to think about, when they really tried to return to the lives they had led before the tornado and had time to think about that night and to wonder, what if they had more equipment, what if they had worked harder. Would they have saved more lives? Would the pain still swallow them up on some days?

Now that the new Station Three was open, Terry's wife Kathy wanted him to spend more time with the family. Lumber and debris still littered the family's yard and work remained undone at their home, work that Terry never got around to because he spent most of his days off helping out the fire district. He knew he needed to give his family more of his time. But he felt guilty for caring for his own when he couldn't save other people's kin. There was one family in Oak Grove he still thought about, a family of three people on Griffis Road. All of them had died. What if he had gotten to them sooner? They were so bad off. Could he and the other rescuers really have saved them? A year had passed, but he couldn't stop wondering. He worried he would think about it even more, now that the station was built and there was no more equipment to be ordered.

Only Chief Love stayed upbeat. The sun beat down on him as he spoke before the dedication crowd and cast away any shadows of sadness from the corners of his eyes. That night, at a party for the firefighters, he danced with the joy of a boozed-up kid. He was straight sober, just full of the good spirits he knew his men needed, that he hoped would rub off on them. Life was gonna get back to normal, he said. Oh yeah, he could guarantee that. "When we get Station Two built," he announced, "that's when we will be back to normal."

No one wanted to admit that the much-hoped-for Station Three wouldn't bring back the life any one knew before the storm. For better and worse, the firefighters were changed, like war veterans who never forgot what they saw on the fields of combat. They were wiser for what they had weathered. They responded to calls with more and better equipment; they had enough backboards to hold blocks of victims, and enough batteries to last a night. They were better neighbors. When the Bessemer Fire Department needed a fire truck, Concord loaned them the best one they had. They took fewer chances, told their wives that they loved them, and in some cases, returned to their religious roots. All of them felt grateful to walk away from the rubble of the storm and to have the past year behind them. But there were wounds that hadn't healed, even though they had assumed that after a year only scars would be left. Grief, as it turned out, didn't know time.

Disaster struck again. One year and nearly one month after the Alabama tornadoes, in the midst of all their healing—Christie Seals had not yet returned to work after a surgery, and Curtis and Cassandra Poe had started fighting again—a deadly spree of ninety-six tornadoes swept through Texas, Oklahoma, Kansas, Nebraska, and South Dakota on May 3, 1999. The hardest hit state was Oklahoma, where sixty-six storms left forty-seven people dead, twenty-six hundred homes destroyed, and eight thousand buildings damaged. The strongest of these killer tornadoes measured F-5 on the Fujita scale and stayed on the ground for more than an hour, obliterating thousands of homes and businesses in its thirty-eight-mile path. University of Oklahoma's Doppler on Wheels gauged the funnel cloud's winds speeds at 318 miles per hour. Moore, South Oklahoma City, Midwest City, and Del City bore the brunt of this storm's fury. Lifelong Tornado Alley residents said it was not like any tornado they had seen before.

The storm blew into Moore shortly after 6 p.m. when the city's fifty thousand residents should have been getting supper on the table instead of cowering in hallways or closets. Earlier that afternoon, Deputy Fire Chief Jerry Doshier had been getting ready for a city council meeting when his wife Karen called and told him that a tornado was on the ground near Lawton. That was more than eighty miles away, so Doshier was not concerned. He asked Karen what was for dinner. Lasagna, she said.

When Doshier arrived at City Hall for the council meeting, he found the fire chief and other city workers hiding. The same storm system that hit Lawton was barreling toward Moore. Spotters reported a massive tornado on the ground and it was not going to spare the city. Without much thought, Doshier ran up to the roof. He was not frightened, and he wanted to see the storm.

Skinny white clouds floated ahead of the funnel cloud like a mist. Then came the tornado, an upside down Christmas tree-shaped cloud that snapped up power lines and transformers in glimmers of red or blue. White lightning flashed in and around the storm's wide girth. Doshier watched as the tornado picked up house after house and exploded it into what looked like glitter, all shiny and bright. A loud hum filled the night, and the twenty-four-year fire veteran shouted descriptions of what he saw and heard into his portable radio. But soon his awe turned to fear as he realized the storm was blowing toward his own home. Karen was going to die, he thought, and cursed himself for not being with her.

He fled the roof, got in his car, and drove as fast as he could to the couple's home. Above him, lightning flickered. At this point, the storm had left his neighborhood, but was continuing to tear through Moore at a speed of forty miles per hour. By the time it was finished with the city, the tornado had wiped away numerous buildings. Doshier did not remember the steady wind that blew around him or the thunder that boomed through the night. He did not recall the houses shredded like paper or the utility poles toppled like twigs. He hollered what he saw into his fire radio, in gripping details that were recorded by emergency dispatchers on a tape that he would not listen to for weeks. At the time, he did not remember what he said or even saying it. His mind was on Karen. It seemed like it took him an hour to reach her. But finally, he did. Buried under a three-foot pile of debris, she had survived the storm. Their home was gone, and in its place sat the mangled remains of four cars and two trailers. Karen had heard the house being ripped from above her and felt the tornado pick up her own body. But somehow, she suffered only bruises. She and Doshier tearfully reunited. They were both alive.

The couple soon moved from the remains of their own home to the corner of their street where they started to set up a medic post with the help of other neighbors and firefighters. People they knew started stumbling out of their homes with gashes, bruises, or even sticks impaled in their bodies. At least six people were dead.

For the next several days, rescue work consumed Doshier. He barely saw his wife and their grown children, all of whom were fine, and he could not begin cleanup at his house. Thoughts of what might have happened, how Karen could have died, filled his mind. He hated himself, because he thought he should have been with her. If she had died, he asked himself, how would he have lived with the guilt? How would he have explained it to the kids?

Relief workers moved into the community with food, water, and hygiene supplies. But Doshier was too busy to stand in line for toothpaste, and he struggled with his insurance company over his claim. Around him, the city lay in shambles. There was so much debris that it seemed useless to try and salvage anything. "Just dig it up and throw it away," Doshier told people.

In Rock Creek, storm spotter Eddie Maxwell and his wife Patricia shook their heads in disbelief as they watched pictures of shattered houses in Moore fill their TV screens. The damage looked so much worse than the devastation in Alabama the year before. It used to be that when Eddie and Patricia saw pictures of storm damage on TV, they watched them with interest and a little bit of awe for nature's power. They felt sympathy for the people who had lost their homes to the furious winds, but it wasn't the same hopelessness they felt for the people they saw on their screen now. It would take years for these survivors to recover, Eddie and Patricia knew, years for them to get over the feeling of being robbed and wanting back what they had before the storm. Generous people would give them things, furniture, clothes, and household items. Beautiful, new things. But all they would want was they could never have again. They would struggle to get back to lives they would never know again, because nothing would ever be the same after a disaster like this rocked their community. Eddie and Patricia started to pray for the survivors.

South of Warrior River Road, across from where a new Station Two was under construction, Concord's Assistant Fire Chief Robbie Miller watched the same pictures of destruction. Having lost his own home a year before, he knew how frightened, angry, and sad were the people on his TV screen. Within days, Robbie and the rest of the Concord firefighters would offer to send workers to help with the cleanup. They also would take $2,000 of the money they had for new equipment and send it to Moore to help the firefighters who lost their homes. Most of the money went to Jerry Doshier and his wife, Karen, who stayed with relatives and in a motel until they found a more permanent place to live. Two other Moore firefighters with damage to their homes received the rest of the cash. Doshier called it a lifesaver.

The gift meant a lot to the Concord firefighters, too. There was a bitter sweetness in finally being able to give, when for so long all they could think about was what nature had taken from them. Life had turned full circle for them when this disaster struck. But it was hard for them not to be tugged by the pictures and stories from Oklahoma, to listen to the anguish of these tornado survivors and to not feel a swelling in their throats. They knew all too well there was nothing anyone could have done to prevent the storm, nothing anyone could have done to stop it. They could only move in after the storm and pick up the pieces. It was their life's work, but sometimes it just wasn't enough.

Matthew Seals made an unexpected move, back to Rock Creek and to the property on Hancock Drive where he lived with Christie and their children before the storm scattered them into the night and pulled them apart from each other. He had a wheelchair-accessible mobile home built with a storm shelter, and he relished his new life as a homeowner. He even bought a riding lawnmower and started landscaping around the house. The property looked different than it did in the days when he lived there with his family. For one, his new house sat in a different spot, actually on a hill, a site that most people in a wheelchair wouldn't choose. But it was fine with Matthew. He saw it as just another challenge for him to conquer. He enjoyed proving to himself what he could do now that he could not walk. No longer an electrician, he had returned to school and worked at Blue Cross and Blue Shield of Alabama in the customer service division. He liked his work, was generally happy, and saw himself as moving on with his life. Occasionally, he found himself giving tornado preparedness tips—advising friends not only to seek shelter in the center of their homes or in their basements, but to wear bicycle helmets as well, in case they get tossed into the night like his family did. He and Christie divorced, but he still worried about her for she often seemed depressed, and he wondered how two people who had been so close could have changed so much because of a tornado.

In the months after the storm, Joseph, Matthew's son from his first marriage, had struggled as well to accept what had happened to the family. He had not been with Matthew and his siblings on the night of the storm, and he could not understand why they had suffered so much.

"It's just not fair, Dad," he had said. "It's just not fair."

"You're absolutely right," Matthew had told him. "You can dwell on that or you can move on."

Matthew realized he had to live by his own advice, too. Since then, he had tried to be more accepting of his circumstances. Matthew believed that Nathan was in heaven and that one day he would see him again. On tough days, days when his personal triumphs weren't enough to cheer him up, he thought about seeing Nathan again. "He's in a better place," he told himself. "And when I get there I am going to look back on this time and know it wasn't as long and as hard as I thought."

There was a job that Assistant Chief Terry Hyche wanted, a job with the fire department in Fairfield, a city northeast of Concord that was home to 12,000 people and to U.S. Steel Corporation. It would be a step up for him and a step away from the daily reminders of the tornado. But he was a little bit nervous, nervous that he wouldn't get the job and nervous about leaving the Concord Fire District if he did. He had worked there for nineteen years, after all.

Nearly two years had passed since the tornado and around Concord's fire stations, nobody mentioned it much anymore. Life really hadn't gotten back to normal, though. Morale seemed down among the firefighters. To Terry, it seemed like some of the younger ones—the new guys who had joined up looking for action after the storm—didn't appreciate how good they had it. They didn't know what it was like to nail up the dry wall in their own station, to fix the engine of a rescue truck themselves. They had the barely used turnout gear, well-working trucks, and all the shiny equipment Terry had spent months ordering. But he watched them treat all of it like they was a pair of their oldest shoes, not even like a consolation prize for having gone to hell and back one spring night. What was worse was that the older guys, the ones who had helped out on the night of the storm, didn't seem as interested in rescue work anymore. Then, one day Curtis Poe told Terry he was thinking about leaving. They shared similar views about the job, and Terry hated the thought of working without his partner.

At the same time, Robbie Miller, the other assistant chief, took a leave of absence to babysit his daughter over the summer and to take a course in real estate. He was even mulling over a move to the Shelby area where the market was hopping. Terry started thinking that maybe it was time for him to go, too. He loved the work of firefighting, the challenge of trying to bring fires under control, putting himself to the test. Running into situations that other people ran from. Lately it felt like he and the other firefighters were just going through the motions. He asked Kathy what she thought.

It was a tough question. Her husband's job was such a mixed blessing, such a point of pride and of pain. She remembered vividly watching him leave on the night of the storm, after the house almost crashed in around them. She knew he was on duty. She knew he had to help the community, and she was proud of him for doing that. But it had been so hard for her to say, "OK, go. We'll be fine" when she hadn't thought they would be.

After the storm, she worried a lot about their oldest boy. Storms still scared David and she wondered if he would ever tire of reading tornado books. But he was no longer frightened of going to school, and he and his brother had rejoined their old classmates from Oak Grove in a temporary classroom at nearby McAdory High School. Freed up from her homeschooling duties, Kathy had taken a job doing the billing at a doctor's office. It was a positive change for her, and she had felt much of her anxiety drain away. She still worried about Terry, though.

At times in their marriage, she had wanted him to give up firefighting. But he never seemed that interested, and she figured he was never going to leave the district. He loved the work too much. She had accepted that so she was surprised when he told her wanted to quit. It was too stressful, he told her, trying to make everything the way it was before the storm. If she agreed, he would give his notice at the end of the fiscal year, a good year with no debts and plenty of money in the bank. All the rebuilding was done. He had gotten the job in Fairfield, and there was no reason to stay. "OK," she told him. "OK." He would be fine. This time, she knew it in her heart.

Terry had put in more years at Concord than many people put in a marriage. Walking away was like divorcing a spouse after the relationship had run its course. But in the end, it was easy. He now accepted that he had done all that he could, on the night of the storm and afterwards. There was nothing left for him to do but to say goodbye.

Two months after the one-year anniversary of the tornado, Melanie and Richie Miller reconciled. She and Christina moved back into the family's Rock Creek home. Melanie and Richie didn't talk too much about their problems. For a long time, he was afraid to ask her why she came back for fear that she would leave again. They set about acting like a family. She unpacked her suitcase, cooked for Richie, and hung up a picture of her husband and their baby that he had taken at the Wal-Mart while they were still separated. It was Melanie's favorite photo.

She didn't like to talk about the tornado, but she still thought about it, and from time to time it filled her dreams at night. When her eyes closed, the tornado blew right towards the house again. Richie and Christina were there, but they didn't know the storm was coming. Melanie was in her car, driving as fast as she could, trying to get home to save them. The storm was coming, faster and faster, but she was picking up more speed, too. She knew she had to get there. If she didn't…then she would wake up.

After the storm, Melanie didn't tell Richie how frightened she was. He would probably laugh at her foolishness, she figured. Richie knew something was eating at Melanie and he didn't know what to do. For months after they reconciled, they lived together without really sharing their thoughts. Then, nearly a year after they got back together and two years after the tornado, the muscular firefighter and his pretty wife separated again and filed for divorce. It was sad, Richie thought, but not a surprise.

Two years after the tornado, Curtis and Cassandra Poe divorced as well. In the end, he figured they had just gotten married too young. They hadn't known who they were or who they wanted to be. After years of fighting, the split was anti-climatic, and as it turned out, divorce was a lot easier than marriage. They agreed to put all their arguments behind them, to work together to look after their two daughters. They made a point to look after each other as well. Curtis wasn't like other ex-husbands, Cassandra told her friends. He always asked if she needed anything.

Cassandra started taking classes for an accounting degree at the University of Alabama at Birmingham and met a nice man at church. Curtis made plans to marry a firefighter he had met on the job at the Birmingham Fire Department.

On his right arm, he got a tattoo, an image of baby angels with his late sister's name, Brandi, inked underneath them. He also started a new job as an exterminator. It wasn't firefighting, but he couldn't turn up his nose at honest work. He earned enough killing bugs to give Cassandra more than he had to in child support. Plus, he worked daylight hours and could see his girls more. He decided to give up his paramedic license, too, and only ran on the fire engine in Birmingham. No more work on the ambulance. He had had it. He liked helping others, but he was tired of "holding hands" with the people who abused the system.

He thought about Nathan Seals from time to time, enough to come to some understanding about the boy's death. He told himself that it had come down to the grace of the good Lord. Nathan's fate wasn't up to some firefighter like him. It was always up to God, who decided this time that the little boy needed to go with him. Curtis wasn't going to win every one. That was all there was to it. He wanted to, hell yes, he really wanted to. But he couldn't. Maybe next time. That was the thing of it. There would always be a next time. Every third day he saw death, and frankly, he was sick of it. He no longer wanted to hold somebody else's fractured child and pray the kid wouldn't die in his arms. It was hard to play God and not win.

When Curtis told Cassandra he would give up his license, she was furious, and some of their last arguments were about his decision. Years before, when they were still together, he had taken her on a call once, a head-on collision right across from the Oak Grove First Baptist Church and about a mile from Station Three. A truck and car had smashed into each other and none of the passengers was wearing a seatbelt. One man lost his nose. It was too much for some of the firefighters on the scene, but Cassandra remembered that Curtis did not lose his cool. He knew exactly what to do and everyone on the scene relied on him, much like they did on the night of the storm.

"Don't give up something you're good at," she begged him. "Please change your mind." He wouldn't, and they finally agreed not to talk about it any more.

One late summer day a few years after the tornado, a storm threatened as Curtis played with his daughters at his parents' house, where he had been living since he and Cassandra had separated. Cassandra had brought Taylor and their youngest, Cori, over that afternoon so Curtis could spend some time with them. It was a hot, dry day in the middle of a drought when dark clouds charged up. Thunder drummed in the sky and the lights went out. Suddenly they were in the midst of the kind of stormy afternoon that brought back many painful memories.

For once, Cassandra felt no dread. In the dark hallway of the house, she sat with Curtis and waited out the storm. They talked about the girls and about Curtis's plans to marry the woman he was dating. They talked about the man Cassandra was seeing, about the storm outside. They talked like they hadn't talked in a long time, like the old friends they really were even though their marriage was over.

It was funny, Cassandra thought later. There they were, hiding from a storm again. But everything was different this time. This man she had loved more than anything, and to whom hard times stuck like the air he breathed, was no longer her husband. He was no longer patching people's wounds for a living, and he might even have been bold enough to say that some of the adrenaline had drained from his hard-charging days. But she wouldn't believe him. He might tell himself that he was fed up with all of the ambulance freeloaders, but when he finally got over Nathan's death, when he really believed that it was up to God and not Curtis Poe, well then, he'd be back saving lives. If time didn't heal all wounds, she thought, it let people walk away from what hurt so much.

Nearly two years after the tornado, Christie Seals returned to work part time after a nine-month recovery following more surgery on her leg. She had trouble standing for very long and still limped when she walked up stairs. For physical therapy, she took an aerobics class designed for senior citizens. As slow as she moved and as much as she had been through, she felt like she fit in well.

After Nathan had died, Christie called the boy's paternal grandmother, whom he had never met. Nathan's biological father had nothing to do with raising the boy, who was later adopted by Matthew, but Christie kept in touch with the woman. Nathan's grandmother was always grateful for the pictures of Nathan that Christie sent her over the years and it broke her heart to hear that her grandson was gone. More than a year after the two women talked, Christie answered the phone one day to a familiar man's voice. It was Nathan's father. He had been watching TV at his home in North Carolina, when an HBO documentary on tornados came on. Christie appeared on the screen in his living room and talked about losing her little boy. On the show, Matthew, the only father Nathan had known, welled up with tears when he talked about how tender-hearted his son was and how he begged God not to have to decide whether to take the boy off life support.

"Tell me about Nathan," Nathan's biological father asked Christie now. "Tell me what I missed."

A few weeks later, he flew into Birmingham, where he met Christie and John Michael and Margaret, who at four and two were the image of their father Matthew. He went to Rock Creek to see where the Seals' house once stood and where his son struggled to stay alive. He drove by Nathan's elementary school in Huey-town. He looked at the pictures of Nathan that friends had rescued after the storm. Then he looked at the last picture of his son, taken in the Children's Hospital emergency room. Quickly he handed it back to Christie. He didn't want to look anymore.

Nathan's father didn't stay in Alabama as long as he had planned. His own grief for the son he never knew came late, but was just as real to him as any parent's grief. It saddened Christie to know that he only knew his son in death. For once, she felt lucky. She had rocked her baby, cut up his food, cheered his Little League team, and held his hand in the hospital as he took his last breaths. She had asked God to let her have him as long as she could, and in the end, it was only for eight years. She wished it could have been forever. But to have never known him at all, to leave on a plane empty-handed and aching like his father, made her thankful for what she had. She would cradle those memories to her, like she would have cradled her boy if he was still with her, and she would go on, knowing that she once had a son who liked to climb trees and make her laugh. When she thought about him now, she smiled.

Final Chapter, Spring 2003

It has been five years since an F-5 tornado plowed through the heart of the Concord Fire District and the lives of the people who lived there, five years since Terry Hyche, Richie Miller, and the others rushed into the night from their battered homes to save their neighbors, and five years since Christie Seals prayed on the rain-soaked ground for someone to come and rescue her family. Half of a decade has passed, and in that time there have been other storms and disasters, as well as unthinkable terrorist acts, and even a war. With each new crisis, I find it hard not to think about the rescue workers in Alabama sitting down to dinner in their rebuilt houses or driving to work on streets that once again look familiar, and I find myself awestruck at the strength and resilience of survivors. We exalt our heroes who save lives in the face of danger—and rightfully so—but most of the victories in life are quiet ones. And some of the bravest people we know are just everyday folk.

After guiding the rescuers through the storm's aftermath, Chief Tim Love left his job with the Concord Fire District in summer of 2002, saying he wanted to spend more time with his family. He continues to work for the Birmingham Fire Department and started a lawn service. He also is teaching his daughter to hunt. He remains the same upbeat and energetic man, but he no longer talks much about the tornado. Assistant Chief Terry Hyche left the Fairfield Fire Department for a better-paying job with the nearby Midfield Fire Department, and in addition, returned to working part time for the Concord Fire District. His oldest son David remains a weather buff, and Terry still believes that David would one day be a meteorologist.

Curtis Poe married Summer Davis, a coworker from the Birmingham Fire Department in September 2000, and returned to his job with the Concord Fire District around the same time. Like Chief Love, he no longer talks about the tornado. Cassandra Poe also remarried in 2000 and gave birth to a little girl, Elizabeth, in 2001. She and her family moved to Montgomery.

Richie and Melanie Miller divorced in 2002. He kept their house in Rock Creek and plans to marry again in July 2003. Richie continues to work for both the Birmingham and Concord fire departments and sees his daughter Christina on his day off. While he remains true to rescue work, he longs for the days before the storm and the fire district's notoriety. "We used to be this Podunk fire department that had to work for everything we got," he says. "Now we don't have to work for anything."

Eddie Maxwell, the volunteer storm tracker, eventually was called back to work in the mines at Jim Walter Resources after being laid off in 1998. He was relieved for the chance to complete his twenty years of service at the company, which would guarantee him a good pension.

On September 23, 2001, Eddie should have been at work in the No. 5 mine with the men on his regular shift, but he had taken the day off. He will be forever grateful for this decision. Twin explosions rocked the mine that Sunday evening in a tragedy that would become the worst mine disaster in the country in seventeen years. Thirteen of the men Eddie had worked with for years perished in a fire that is still under investigation. Afterwards, Eddie gave up his volunteer position with the Concord Fire District. When he was on duty, he often thought about the miners who had burnt to death, and he realized he no longer had the heart for rescue work. On a happier note, Patricia's depression eased in the years after the tornado, and the family also welcomed their first grandchild, Alana Marie.

Christie Seals continues to cope with reoccurring medical problems, including chronic pain in her left leg. She left and returned to her job at Children's Hospital numerous times, each time vowing to continue her work there without letting her physical pain or grief interfere. But she finally left her job at the hospital for good in October 2002. She barely supports her family on disability payments, but hopes one day to return to school to be trained in a profession that isn't as physically demanding as nursing. Depression continues to plague her, and she still misses Nathan greatly.

Matthew Seals still lives in Rock Creek, but thinks he will look for a home closer to his job at Blue Cross and Blue Shield of Alabama; he no longer feels he has something to prove by living in what once was the disaster zone. He, too, misses Nathan, but the tornado has become a memory for him. "Life goes on and we're making it," Matthew says. "By the grace of God, go we."

A Note on Sources

Much of the information for this book came from interviews I conducted in the days and months after the April 8 storm. The American Red Cross sent me to Alabama within twenty-four hours of the tornado's touchdown, and I visited the communities of Oak Grove and Rock Creek four subsequent times. The level of detail the survivors in this book were able to recall may seem unbelievable to anyone who hasn't lived through a disaster. But this tornado was a once-in-a-lifetime event for these victims, and any relief worker could tell you that a survivor's need to talk about his or her experiences is a vital part of the recovery process. This telling and retelling of personal disaster stories makes it easy for a journalist to verify facts. However, there were numerous experts as well as regular folks who provided information or directed me to other sources during the reporting process.

Much of the information concerning tornadoes, weather, disaster preparedness, relief work, and the emotional effects of disasters came from a year I spent flying to and reporting about disasters as a writer for an American Red Cross Web site, DisasterRelief.org. During that time, I received a thorough education from my Red Cross coworkers, as well as disaster experts at the Federal Emergency Management Agency and other agencies, who never hesitated to share as much information as they could with a reporter. Information on the deadly 1998 spring tornado season came from my experiences covering the disasters as they happened, and also from a presentation that Joseph Schaefer, director of the Storm Prediction Center in Norman, Oklahoma, made during a tornado forum held August 1998 in Washington, D.C. Dr. Schaefer generously furnished me a copy of his remarks, entitled, "Bad, But It Could Have Been Worse."

Diane Black of Children's Hospital in Birmingham supplied information on the number of children treated at their outstanding facility in the aftermath of the storm and allowed me to tour the hospital. Nez Calhoun of the Jefferson County Board of Education detailed the history of the Oak Grove School for me. Russell Carter of Texas Tech University provided the facts and figures about the wind engineering research team that visited Alabama in the days after the tornado. Greg Jaffe of the Wall Street Journal was on assignment at the National Weather Service on April 8 and sent me the subsequent article he wrote about the experience, and he shared with me additional insights about that night. In addition, Brian Peters, warning coordination meteorologist at the National Weather Service near Birmingham, answered endless questions about the storm and its aftermath.

Information on the May 1999 tornado spree that struck Oklahoma came from the National Weather Service, the Oklahoma Department of Civil Emergency Management, and interviews with Deputy Fire Chief Jerry Doshier of the Moore Fire Department in Oklahoma. Chief Jim Scholl of the Cranston Heights Fire Department in Delaware recalled the story behind the fire truck that was sent to Alabama. The Alabama Emergency Management Agency furnished the figures on the number of fatalities and the number of injured on April 8. Chaplain Ted Wilson of the Oklahoma City Fire Department generously agreed to be interviewed, and spoke both candidly and eloquently about the effects of the 1995 bombing on his coworkers.

0-595-27706-3